Yes! You Can Do It!

The Young Woman's Guide to Starting a Fulfilling Career

NANCY WILHELMS

YES! YOU CAN DO IT!
The Young Woman's Guide to Starting a Fulfilling Career
Smoke Tree Press/January 2021
All rights reserved
Copyright © 2021 by Nancy Wilhelms

Cover and interior design by Self-Publishing Lab

Back cover photograph by Jim Paussa

Permission requests should be addressed in writing to:
Nancy Wilhelms, PO Box 2856, Basalt, CO 81621
or to Nancy@NancyWilhelms.com

ISBN 978-1-7364433-0-9

Legal Disclaimer

To Harriet Fisher, my mom,
who always said to me, "Yes! You can do it!"

Contents

Preface

This book will make you think about who you are and what you want. It will help you throw aside notions placed in your head by others, especially parents and family members, about what you should do with your life. It will provide worksheets and personal profile materials to help you think, analyze and project your future. And it will reinforce what you know in your gut about yourself and about what will work for you and make you smile.

Placed throughout the book you'll find profiles and quotes from professional women that I know and admire. They are successful in their careers and lives and believe that you can be, too. One of them, my niece Colby Fisher Dailey, worked with my husband and me in our marketing firm early in her career and encouraged me to tell my stories, like I did with her, and to write this book.

While I have been fortunate in that, throughout my life and career, I have been able to take advantage of some unique opportunities, it's my hope that what I share here is universal in nature and can help you get on an excellent career path for yourself, regardless of your circumstances or background. Even if you are not able to relate to some of the examples, I hope that you can take away the lessons learned from them.

When I began my career I was a minority: A young woman in a business world that did not welcome women. I was one of many firsts... the first female photographer to show work at the Milwaukee Press Club; the first woman granted a bank mortgage in a rural Wisconsin town; the first woman who did not punch a time clock in the 90-year history of a particular 4,500-employee corporation; and more. Today, women in business are not a minority and instead dominate fields in which then they were neither present nor welcomed years ago.

I hope that this book leads you down challenging, exciting paths and that you enjoy the experience...for a lifetime!

Introduction

My first three jobs set the tone for my career

It all began in Milwaukee, though I really didn't intend to stay. Arriving from art school in Providence with everything I owned packed into a red Jeep with my bike hanging on the back, I was stopping home to see Mom, throw some things in her attic and head out for what I imagined to be my new life in the Pacific Northwest. But a case of mononucleosis stalled me and there I was.

I decided to practice job hunting before I hit the road for my upcoming "real life." This was merely a speed bump.

Seeing myself as a budding Ansel Adams or Richard Avedon, I connected with photographer after photographer—commercial photographers, documentary photographers, portrait photographers—and anything in between. But there were no jobs. Not one. Not even at the big studios. Annie Leibovitz had not yet hit the scene, and perhaps they were reluctant to take a chance on me.

Not defeated, I decided to try something else that involved art. Anyone who watched could see that the local TV news sets

1

were cheerless and outdated. Through persistence I landed an appointment with a station manager and explained what I might do to give them a new look. I must have hit a sweet spot because he hated the sets, wanted something fresh and hired me on a contract. It was a six-week job that got me started in the world of work. Finally, I had money in my pocket.

For my first two weeks on the job I worked as a stagehand to learn how the cameras were used in the studios, and how the light influenced the skin tones, the colors of clothing on the talent and the weather map. I was the "new girl" in a world that was then full of men. Today, more women are in TV and news, but then, I was a novelty. I went on to design modular sets that were later part of their brand. "Oh my gosh," I thought. "They believed me, and we made this work!"

Prior to getting the TV job, I had dropped off a resume at one of the big three breweries, Schlitz, seeking to join their photography department. The human resources director advised that there were no openings, but the next morning at 8:00 am the phone rang with their vice president of marketing inviting me for an interview in two short hours. I was in my pajamas but quickly dressed and headed out the door. When I arrived, I found that the VP wasn't the least bit interested in me and there were no jobs. Instead, I answered his questions about a former colleague who taught in the art department at the University of Colorado, my alma mater. I was thinking this was all a big bust.

And then the VP gave me a pearl...he passed me off to the photo team. In addition to knowing how to shoot beer in every possible light and dimension—with foam, poured from the bottle, poured from the glass, poured from a pitcher, coming out of a tap—they were fun, friendly and encouraging. They knew all of the photographers and marketing people in town. After meeting with them, I was ready to network. But I still didn't have a job.

I'm glad I ignored those who said I didn't have a chance

I'd already decided to look into what I imagined to be the most exciting place in Milwaukee to work, Milwaukee Summerfest. Ten days of fun and music at the lakefront, it sounded just right to me. However, the Schlitz photo team warned, "Sure, go for it. But you'd need to be the mayor's daughter to get a job there." I certainly wasn't the mayor's daughter, but I did go for it.

At 3:00 on a Friday afternoon, exactly the wrong time to job hunt, I stopped by in person to drop off a resume. "We don't have any jobs," I was told by the executive secretary. "But have a seat and let me share this with my boss." Her boss came out and told me the same thing, "no jobs," and invited me to join a "cake and beer" birthday party in the small offices they occupied.

"Oh, Nancy," he called after me as I was headed out the door, "we do have a job and it's yours if you want it." Sly fox... he had been observing me to see how I interacted with his staff and whether I'd be a good fit. That afternoon I became Program Manager of the 1972 Milwaukee Summerfest, responsible for staging throughout the grounds, including the Main Stage. Aretha Franklin, the Doors, Ray Charles, BB King, Glen Campbell, Loretta Lynn, Charley Pride, Arlo Guthrie and many more appeared during our ten festival days, and all performed on my Main Stage.

Was it magic, charisma, camaraderie that landed me this job? No. It was being at the right place, at the right time, with the right resume and a decision to push forward to see what was out there! Bullheaded me. I forgot to listen to those who told me that no one could get a job there.

So, getting started in my career, I landed both jobs, the TV set design job for six weeks followed by the Summerfest job that lasted four months. The pay was subsistence, but the experiences and opportunities were huge.

Summerfest at that time provided only seasonal work for most of its staff. After Summerfest, my boss arranged an interview for me with Tom, an ad agency owner, and it was at Tom's agency, Communique, where I started my "forever career."

Move quickly if you make mistakes and end up in the wrong spot

However, after Summerfest and before the ad agency, I did wander off the path a bit. I thought I had the right job from an ad I'd found in the newspaper as marketing director for a dinner theater. I interviewed and took the job, not having met my employer. "You'll love him," said the gentleman in charge of hiring.

This job did not come through friends or referrals. And it came with a lot of urgency, as I was pressed by the personnel man to make up my mind fast and appear the next day. I had no time to check out the company and its reputation.

When I showed up the first day, things didn't feel right. First, there was no one to welcome me. Then, I learned that the boss rarely darkened the doorway and when I did meet him, I knew right away he was not the right boss for me. He was the big boss with no time to teach, train, set expectations or even talk about the job. I had done exactly the wrong thing: I took a job for which I had no experience with no mentor in sight. And, I went against myself; this job required me to be downtown after dark in a location I'd rather avoid.

At the dinner show the very first evening, I gracefully resigned my brand-new marketing position. "Why," asked the man who hired me. "I don't believe that I'm the right fit." No kidding. I was jobless again and that only took one day.

Landing my first long-term career job, I could finally breathe

Luckily, my boss at Summerfest had arranged that interview with Tom. I called and he invited me to meet with his partner for an interview.

When I stepped into the cozy basement offices of that ad agency for the job interview, I didn't know how lucky I was. A 22-year-old recent college graduate, I had dropped into a welcoming, creative environment in a small company run by an outstanding writer and excellent teacher. He would place his trust in me and open a doorway to a creative world that became my career. Under his tutelage, I produced radio spots and brochures, worked with designers and photographers, edited magazines, hired stylists and models and was challenged daily. I landed in exactly the right place for me.

My career beginning was simple. It included two short-term jobs with relatively low pay that I took for the experience, contacts and opportunities they'd provide, a very good gamble.

From there, I went on to my first real career job at the ad agency, where I began part-time and within four weeks was moved to full time. While I thought that I was to be a photographer, these were the steppingstones to the most exciting career, the right career for me, that I could ever have.

Of course, I eventually left the ad agency and learned that not all bosses or jobs are that great (although most jobs are not as dicey as that job at the dinner theater).

Since that time, I have hired and worked with many young women who didn't know where to start, what a career is all about or where they'd fit. I am writing to share what I know to help you find the best start for you.

Why should you take my advice?

Before diving into this book you probably want to know a few things about me, to convince you that I'm qualified to help *you* think through all of this. In my career, I:

- Ran the main stage for a 10-day music festival
- Worked for a small ad agency
- Served as Manager of Communications for a Fortune 500 company
- Created a photo studio and photographed the rodeo circuit
- Was the marketing director for a Las Vegas hotel and casino
- Worked with a Governor of Nevada as his Administrative Assistant and Press Secretary
- Founded and was CEO of a marketing communications firm that served large corporate clients for 25 years
- Headed an internationally-known nonprofit arts center

Through it all, I have hired dozens of employees, people who perhaps were a bit like you.

I got off to a strong start in my career because I had a mentor, my mother. Mom was a fashion designer, a working woman in an era when they were rare. So when I arrived on the basement doorstop of the ad agency, I already knew the basics of how to work. Though I was a rookie, I was a prepared rookie.

In my world of work, I had an essential goal. I wanted my life to be exciting, fulfilling and free of bosses. But at age 22, I knew I lacked the skills to start in business for myself. I had watched my mother work hard every day, taking only two weeks off per year to be with us and enjoy new things. Once, she was abruptly interrupted during our precious Colorado summer vacation by a boss who couldn't get something done on his own and called her back to Wisconsin. I fully respected her but wanted my work life to be different.

Getting your first excellent job is harder now than ever, and a greater dependence on technology instead of face-to-face interaction complicates what is already a difficult process. Young women tell me they are eager to work but often confused and perplexed as to where to start and how to keep going. *Yes! You Can Do It!* is a practical, real-world guidebook that addresses these challenges. I hope that it will help you venture forward on the right livelihood for you, full of accomplishment, enjoyment and success.

Chapter 1
Identify and Value Your Passion

Build your career around something you love, and it will be a
"forever career" for you.

Do you believe that you can have a fulfilling career while living a fulfilling life? I believe the answer is yes—and by the time you finish this book, I hope you agree that you are in charge of your career future and your rich, rewarding life. Let's get started!

Believe in yourself and enjoy your sense of adventure

Honestly, when I got started, I really did not know what I wanted to do. I had a good education and started looking for photography jobs, but none were available. I knew that I loved art and design. Live music and fun events have always been exciting to me. Somehow, I trusted that a combination of job experiences could come together into a fantastic career. And they have.

You don't have to know what you want to do. Sometimes, it's enough to just know what you love and what makes you smile and head for that. Your passion will reveal itself in the choices you make.

Trust what feels right

One of my favorite quotes is from the Cheshire Cat in *Alice in Wonderland*. Alice is bustling down the road and spots the Cheshire Cat draped across a tree limb above the road. "Which way shall I go?" she asks. He responds by asking her where she's going. "I really don't know," she replies. "Then what does it matter what road you take to get there?" he grins down at her.

What is it that you do that when you do it, you don't get tired? For me it is working in the darkroom, processing my photos. What is it for you? The answer may provide a directional clue to your path. Don't expect to find a big signpost in the middle of the forest pointing you there. But there are clues.

Trust what feels right. Your career may connect directly with your passion, or your passion may be separate but somehow connected. What lights you up? You will know for the rest of your life when you're "on" and when you're "off," and you will learn to value that.

Yes, you'll make some mistakes along the way. I know that I certainly did. But you'll learn from them and move on.

Get started on the right path

Getting off to the right start in your career search can lead to a lifetime of challenge and excitement, keep a sparkle in your eye and a lilt in your voice forever. I want that for you. In some ways, it's the harder route, working against the grain of taking the easy opportunities. I am hoping to convince you to take the right opportunities for you, no matter how daunting they seem at the time.

For many years my life has been a whirlwind of activity and a daily joy. With this book, I want to help you create your dream life, too.

Start with a simple worksheet

I've developed a simple worksheet for you (see Appendix 1, "Personal Inventory," also available for download at www. NancyWilhelms.com) to help you keep sight of who you are and what you love. Every time you are tempted to get on a career track or apply for a job and interview, just pull it out and fill it in. This worksheet will help you evaluate why you might be right for this job and why it may be good for you.

If you proceed on to an interview, the worksheet will help you talk with your interviewer about what you will bring to their company or organization. Filling it out may bring up good questions that you can ask. Or, conversely, filling out the form may show you that the job or opportunity is all wrong and may help you avoid wasting your or the employer's time by interviewing for a job that you know you don't want.

Be uniquely you

To others, my career appears to be a checkerboard, but for me, the thread of my passion runs throughout. I have always loved the creative world. I studied art in college and then attended art school. In some careers I was the artist, a photographer, and in others, I directed or coordinated the artists. Always, except once, I have worked in an artistic or creative environment, and the one time I didn't, I failed. I simply didn't belong there, and everyone knew it. I was miserable.

You'll find that many careers offer tremendous flexibility. Some of them enable you to travel, meet with people in all walks of life and experience many things. Some are in nature and the outdoors, in urban, mountain or ocean areas. Other careers are home-based, office-based or facility-based. Who are you and what makes you smile? You want to head there.

While your parents, relatives and friends believe they know what you should do, do they really know you? That's the important piece to consider when taking advice. You can always listen to your Aunt Tilly and say, "I'll think about that," so she knows you heard her, but nod your head and then do what's right for you.

I'm guessing that you are curious, excited and a bit fearful about starting your career. I know I was. I remember my first interviews. You'll remember yours. And you'll know when your arrow hits the target.

Use creativity if you need to work now while you continue to seek your ideal job

Let's face it, sometimes you may not have good choices and having a job is bowing to pressure to simply put bread on the table. That's life. But through it all, you can and must continue to pursue opportunities that dovetail with your eventual career goals. You may need to work at one job while you seek another for your ultimate career start. By using your creativity to get in or close to the environment you seek, you can learn while you work, and begin to network, too.

Imagine that you need to continue working in your current job or get a job right away to keep things going or pay off debt while you are looking for the real job, the forever job you seek. Let's say your goal is to work as a private wealth manager with high-net-worth clients at a financial institution. Would you consider applying for a waitressing job in a downtown restaurant where financial services people dine? You can meet some of them, observe how they dress, learn the vocabulary they use and start to feel comfortable in their universe while you continue your dream job search. You will have more tools when you interview and could meet someone that will be very interested in your goals and business degree. When you get into the universe of people in the career field you seek, you multiply your knowledge of the field, and start to increase your chances of success.

Use your moxie to get moving

I have met many women (and count myself among them) who started in one city because it was easy to get going, especially when living at home with parents, and later made a career move to the location of their dreams.

One friend was in snowy Maine working as a graphic designer until she heard "*California Dreaming*" by the Mamas & Papas on the radio. She dreamed of surfing and packed up and left with no job prospects and no contacts. Today she lives and works three blocks from the beach in San Diego.

Living the young career woman life in Minneapolis, Jennifer Slaughter left her uptown lifestyle to head for a small town in Colorado. How she arrived is fascinating. She credits the "informational interview" with helping her get the job and fuel her passion. We'll catch up with her later.

Moving into your dream is what this book is about. Don't be hard on yourself or expect to achieve success overnight. That's not how it usually works. Starting on a path that truly reflects who you are enables you to cocoon for a while as you get started and later burst out like a butterfly. It will take time, focus and intention, and it'll be worth every hour you spend.

Recognize that when you love what you do, it's not work

When you discover your personal calling, you'll know it. I want to help you find it. "When you love what you do, it's not work," many say—and it's true.

The experiences you explore will propel you many different directions, possibly with choices you never thought possible. Just get started with a good sense of who you are and what you love, and you'll find out for yourself.

As Woody Allen said, "Eighty percent of success is showing up." So, get started!

Chapter 2
Prepare to Look for a Great Job

*Start with YOU, what you are looking for and
how to set your goals to get it!*

Clarity makes a difference

The tools you need to get started on a fulfilling career are right
in front of you and easily available. When you focus on basic
things, you'll find that you are well-equipped and ready to go
forward with your ideas.

First, you need to really have a good understanding of you
and what works for you (and what does not). When you have that
clarity, you will look only in the right places and not waste time
looking in the wrong ones. You'll soon find that it takes as much
time, effort and energy to apply and interview for the wrong job
as it does for the right one, so why waste time on the wrong ones?

Ask yourself and continually return to these two basic
questions:

- What field or industry do I really want to work in?
- Who do I know that can open doors for me?

Read on and you will discover tools to help you gain more clarity about where to go and the possibilities there, and, importantly, how to network and nail real interviews with real people who have the potential to help or hire you.

Start with YOU

Understanding what will really work for you and make you smile will launch you into your career.

A school career counselor suggested to ocean rower Roz Savage, 2010 National Geographic Adventurer of the Year, that she be a hairdresser. Thankfully, Roz ignored this advice.

My own high school counselor blocked all of my attempts to take art classes because, as she said, "You are too smart for art." When I arrived at college and declared an art major, I was far, far behind. Yet love of art has been the focal point of my career.

I have met too many unhappy doctors, lawyers, stockbrokers and high-tech executives. They are good people in the wrong roles because their parents or others thought they were "perfectly suited" for those careers, when they would have been happier as tennis coaches, graphic designers, musicians and salespeople. But they were made to feel that anything other than the "big professional success" was not worthy of them. I was married to a man who believed he'd be a total failure if he was a basketball coach, his dream since he was a boy, instead of a private practice attorney. It took a terrible toll on his happiness.

Can you make solid, honest and realistic choices for yourself? Can you make career choices that make you happy? Yes! You may have to do some work, though.

Set your own goals, as no one else's will work for you

Annie always told herself that she was going to be architect. She's intelligent and creative and her father was an architect. Annie pretended to accept her family's false goal to keep them off her back. What it did though, was give Annie a distorted sense of direction instead of allowing her to pursue her dreams.

Annie loves working with people and using her big personality in marketing. Friends commented on how outstanding she was when behind the counter at a Gucci outlet store in the nearby community. "Oh, I love working in luxury goods," Annie said. With her college education, professional presence and experience in retail, Annie can work her way up in the luxury goods industry, which requires everything from store managers and event planners to corporate VPs. In this career, Annie can feel like herself, relaxed and not headed into years of education and years of frustration at her drafting table. When she corrected her course to pursue her interests, Annie began to smile again and took off in her new career.

Strive for the joy of work and learning. Don't just work!

This is your life. Career decisions are your decisions. You may want to use your career to make the world a better place through social justice, medicine or environmental action in a very demanding career. Or you may want to support yourself in a casual lifestyle, be with your children as they grow or travel to exotic places when you are young.

Create a vision for yourself and work on it steadily and persistently. Give yourself lots of time to learn. "You have enough time to do what you need to do...always," says sculptor Arlene Shechet.

This is *your* time to choose an exciting and fulfilling path, so give it the energy and relentless effort required to do it right. That doesn't mean that you have to know exactly where you are going. It simply means that when you hit the fork in the road, you'll have perspective and know the heart path for you. If you are just starting down a path, see it as a golden opportunity to create something truly special and all yours.

Be realistic. If you love the outdoors and the ocean and are skilled at computer programming, is there a job in computers that may take you someplace exciting, like working on a research ship? Or perhaps you like solitude, artistic work and details in a way that may take you to an artist's studio manager's job. Put together some creative combinations. It's your life and you've got to have fun, satisfaction and pride. You won't settle for less!

Don't be afraid to look off the grid, interviewing for the unexpected things that come up. Have no fear about creating your own job when you see opportunities that others don't.

Start your career search by taking a fresh look at your existing skills

Stop right now, go to the "Personal Inventory" in Appendix 1 and make a list of what you know how to do. This is not a resume, it's a list. Once you are finished, you will see that you have a whole basket of skills and experience to bring to an employer. These are the skills that you will load into your resume and discuss in your interviews, especially if you are new to work and have limited work experience.

Perhaps you are an excellent babysitter or know calligraphy. Maybe you can load a stock trailer with cattle or operate a SKILSAW®. Or it's possible you went to Honduras on a church youth mission or are an expert at running online meetings or writing code. There's a long list of you.

Using the chart, write a description of what each skill exemplifies. For example:

- Babysitting = responsibility, problem-solving
- Calligraphy = interest in art and cultures, precision
- Loading a stock trailer = good at handling animals; patience, persistence, perseverance

Then go on from there. Shine a new light on yourself and the experiences, attributes and qualities you will bring to your employer. Don't stop until you have listed at least ten things you know how to do and the skills they require. This list of skills will help you see some of the things you can offer an employer and give you information you can share in your job interviews.

Recognize the value of your summer and school-year jobs

Have you ever wondered if you were just wasting time in your summer job? Others around you were enrolled in summer school, plugging ahead to graduate early or head to graduate school. Some lucky kids got to go to Europe or Morocco. Some went on missions to places like Vietnam, Thailand and India. Many took jobs with landscape companies or as waitresses or temporary helpers. Some went to the beach and didn't work at all.

The reality is, the jobs you have held so far have not been a waste of your time. As you are creating this personal inventory, it's important that you don't overlook all of the things you have learned at summer and school-year jobs.

For example, when I was 16 I got my first summer job. We were in Colorado on vacation at the ranch we went to each summer. One of the waitresses had to leave early and the owner asked if I would like to stay and take her place. My mother said okay, and that was the start of my very young career.

The next summer I returned as a children's counselor, and day after day I learned that work can really be fun. I was paid for lifeguarding, playing capture the flag and kick-the-can and teaching riding. Throughout college I'd head back to the ranch each summer to work and learn.

And learn I did. I learned how to find gates and ways home when I was lost with a whole ride of children behind me. I learned how to make horses go over things they don't want to. I learned how to be gentle and firm at the same time because I was in charge and, ultimately, I was responsible. I learned how to administer first aid and I earned my junior lifesaving certificate at college because those were the skills I needed to have to be comfortable on the job.

These same skills apply to my work every day. I know how to find a way to do or deliver what seemingly can't be done. I'm capable of taking employees and clients where they don't want to go. I take responsibility for my actions and decisions and for those of my company, standing behind them and making right what is wrong. I make sure that many workers on my jobsite or in my offices are current in first aid. Oh my gosh, these are my summer job skills!

My 16-year-old waitressing skills have also paid off. Not only did I gain an understanding of customer service and how to deal with demanding customers, I also learned how a 5-star resort sets its tables and how a well-set dining room looks and operates. Decades later, when I found myself overseeing a cafe as part of an arts center and serving as hostess for deluxe fundraising events, this knowledge was priceless.

You possess strong messages for employers to hear. "I know how to do this" and "this is how I will be able to put that to work for you" is music for their ears. You have learned a lot. It's up to you to recognize and share it.

Understand how to use and communicate the benefits of your real-world experience

One of the most important things prospective employers look for in an entry-level hire is the simple one—other than go to school, what has this person done with their life? Employers are looking for all of the basics plus *real world* experience. That's experience gained with co-workers and the public or teaching or traveling.

Frequently they are looking for a team player, and that's something to emphasize as you seek a starting job. A soccer player who coaches during summer breaks will get an employer's attention. Someone who has worked as a census taker, done construction work or volunteered for a community food bank will be of interest.

Likely they are looking for good people skills, so someone who has been a caregiver for elderly relatives, worked in a hospital or nursing home or stayed home to babysit younger siblings has equally valid experience.

An applicant who has traveled, responsible for caring for themselves and making their own way, will be a good candidate for work in certain careers.

Think deeply about what you have done so far in your life. You likely have some valuable real-world experience that is uniquely yours that you can talk about to show the skills you have and what you have learned.

Identify your strong career choices with the "Personal Career Map"

Mapping what careers will make you happy and where you might fit will help you understand where to start and also, what new skills you need to acquire to get the jobs you want.

The Personal Career Map is a simple tool that will help you be honest with yourself about specific careers and job openings. This chart is based upon desirability and probability. The reasoning is simple: When desirability and probability come together, you have a good match for a professional career. When they are far apart, you may be dreaming, but you're dreaming too far in the ozone. For success, you'll need to get back to reality or change something in the equation to make it work.

To get started on your Personal Career Map, visit Appendix 2 at the back of this book. A downloadable template of the Personal Career Map is also available at www.NancyWilhelms. com.

For this exercise make a list of all of the possible careers or jobs you are considering. Also list those that are in your dreams. This is a tool to see where you can go and what it will take to get there. You can map several careers on one page and compare them for your current likelihood of success.

This tool asks you to write down jobs you believe you would like and then take a realistic look at the probability of your getting them or getting started toward them. If you don't have the skills or experience for a particular career, it will show up. But that is also a starting point for knowing what you might need to do to get a foothold toward that career. Start on your Personal Career Map now to get a head start on your dream career.

Understand what employers are looking for

You'll need to develop the job search tools that communicate how hiring YOU will benefit THEM.

Amongst the highly successful women I know, five key traits have kept them moving forward. They are:

- **Courage** - The ability to act beyond your fears
- **Authenticity** - Being true to yourself at all times, not morphing into someone else in order to impress or achieve success
- **Flexibility** - Adapting to do the hard work that no one else wants to do

- **Self-confidence** – Trusting and sticking by your decisions
- **Integrity** – Acting with sincerity and staying true to your values in all circumstances

Give some thought to yourself and your life and make a list of times and events where you exemplified each of these traits. Now list some examples to share with employers. "I knew I had courage when...." "I demonstrated loyalty when...." Appendix 3 contains a worksheet, "Examples About Me," to help you think these things through. You can also download the worksheet at www.NancyWilhelms.com.

Because employers seek someone who will make their organization even better through teamwork, they are also looking for these qualities in their new hires:

- **The ability to work collaboratively**
- **The ability to think creatively**
- **The desire to keep learning**

When you approach an interview with real examples in mind as to how you creatively solved a problem for a team you worked on, or what you did in collaboration with others that made a difference, you are walking in the door prepared.

Think about the basic skills that most jobs require

Today, most every job from waitress to astronaut requires the deft handling of computers. You will likely be required to know Microsoft Word, Excel and PowerPoint, or Google Docs, Google Sheets and Google Slides, and know them inside out. Whether your first job requires these skills or not, you will use them for the rest of your life (or until a new technology comes along that replaces them). If you need to bump up your computer skills, take a course now.

If you go to work in a specialty area like resort management, fund raising/development or tax accounting, you will be asked to learn software developed for that particular endeavor. Should you interview with an employer that requires the use of specialty software that you don't know, offer to learn immediately upon being hired.

If you are targeting a career in communications, marketing or public relations, you must be a master at social media and know how to access and interpret analytics, as well.

Regardless of what career you are pursuing, basic communications skills are golden. This includes reading, writing and presenting skills, as well as the ability to create financial tools such as spreadsheets. You will use these to build reports, work with your teams and communicate daily.

Continue to learn as you go. It's a lifetime process.

Chapter 3
Prepare the Right Tools

Once you have the right tools in your quiver,
looking for a job becomes easy!

Focus on the tools for success in your job search

You will need a:
- Resume
- Cover letter
- LinkedIn profile
- Website (optional)
- Portfolio and samples (depending on your experience)

Know what employers look for on resumes

Employers want to see your resume because prior jobs are an indicator of who you are. Activities and interests are also clues. If you trekked the Appalachian Trail, that's a clue, though you don't need to have done exotic things to get an interviewer's attention. Let's say you spent last summer taking care of a disabled grandparent. While not as exciting, that counts, and may count even more depending on the career.

Areas of interest reveal what you love. If you play oboe or tennis, list that passion. Share what excites you.

For most jobs, several qualified candidates are in the pool. Any one of them can do the work. Assuming that you are qualified for the job, your challenge is to stand out. But be truthful, always.

In creating your resume be sure to match some of the words in your resume to the keywords that may appear in the job descriptions to which you are responding. Often, especially with large companies, the first pass at resume screening is done by a computer that is simply searching for those words. For example, if the job description includes the words "self-motivated," and those words, "self-motivated" appear on your resume, you heighten the chances that your resume will be selected by the automated system.

Write your resume to get the job you want

If you've decided to apply for jobs as a Forest Ranger, write a resume that showcases the skills that will get you hired into that field. You've already identified them in your Personal Inventory and Personal Career Map.

Your goal is to make your resume interesting so that you get noticed. Your resume will include the basics of your education, jobs you've held and how to contact you. It will also include special achievements or awards and a short list of your personal activities and interests.

Keep your resume short and smart. You're just starting out, so prospective employers are not expecting too much. They just want to know your potential. As you begin your career, I recommend that you keep your resume to one page.

Avoid using a font that is smaller than 10 points. Summarize your experiences giving enough information, but not details. You'll cover those details in your interviews.

Make sure that your resume contains lots of "white space" so that it's not filled with so much text that it looks like a black page. Your resume will showcase your organizational abilities and show whether or not you have professionalism and understand how business correspondence should look. It should be neat, clean and easy to read...and not at all flowery. You may want to show your resume to trusted family members or friends to get feedback.

A sample resume is at Appendix 4 and also available for download at www.NancyWilhelms.com.

Customize your cover letter for each job

The next career search tool that you'll need is a good cover letter. Andrew Carnegie is famous for saying, "It's not how they are interested in you that matters. It's your interest in them." Remember that sentence as you write your cover letter and as you interview. The more you know about the employer, how you will fit and why you want to belong there, the better your cover letter and interview will be, and the better your chances for getting the job.

Always send both a resume and a cover letter. Just sending a resume looks like you're "shot gunning" with no particular commitment to the company or the job you're seeking. Recruiters will not be interested in you if you don't take the time to be interested in the job or company for which they are hiring.

The reality is, quite often the recruiter sorts applications very simply. Resumes with cover letters go to the top of the pile and resumes without cover letters go to the bottom. Just like I mentioned for your resume, be sure to include key words and phrases from the job ad in your cover letter, too.

The way to success in this area is to do your homework in order to know as much about your prospective employer as you can before you write the cover letter or appear for an interview. A meaningful cover letter is a must because cover letters will get you the job more often than your resume.

If your cover letter is written for the person who has the job opening and addresses why you are the right person for the job, you get into the running. In order to pull this together you will want to fill in the "Job Interview Worksheet," an amazing tool to match you with your job opportunities. A template is available in Appendix 5 at the back of this book and for download at www.NancyWilhelms.com. This worksheet will help you find out all that you can in order to determine if this company or job is a good fit for you and your interests.

Once you fill out this worksheet you can use the information you learned to help craft your cover letter. For example:

- **Do deep research on the company and reflect this in the letter:** "I see that you are expanding into Chicago, where I attended college at X."

- **Connect your experience with the deep research:** "Given your company's new ventures into screen-sharing technology, I believe that my interning experience with XYZ Company will benefit your marketing program."
- **Show how your background, interests and experience will benefit the company:** "As a champion NCAA sailor, I learned to move quickly and solve problems in a flash and will bring that skill to this job."

Your goal will be to connect to this company in your cover letter. This is not about "I this" and "I that" but about THEM and what you will bring to the job that will benefit THEM. Once you communicate on that level, you get job offers!

Spoiler alert: One cover letter does not fit all. You must write a fresh cover letter that specifically addresses each job opportunity and company.

Use the Personal Inventory, Personal Career Map and the Job Interview Worksheet templates to comfortably prepare to be successful in any job interview.

Create a strong LinkedIn profile

LinkedIn is the leading online tool used by recruiters and hiring managers. In their promotional literature, LinkedIn claims that 70% of recruiters refer to LinkedIn when making a hire, and I believe it. Having a profile on LinkedIn gives you an immediate online presence. When prospective employers do a Google search, which is likely the first thing they will do when they have your name in front of them, you'll show up because LinkedIn is a powerful tool to put you and your credentials online and help you appear on Google's first page.

LinkedIn enables you to write a strong personal profile that shows who you are and why you are unique, and to build your own personal brand online. You can (and should!) upload your professional photo as well. And LinkedIn is free. While a premium version is available for a fee, it's not needed for the site to work well for you.

LinkedIn is an incredible networking tool. Having "connections" is like having a personal contacts list of people that you have talked with about your career. Through LinkedIn you stay in front of each other on the site and can re-connect when you have news or questions. The site enables you to follow companies and individuals, as well as job postings, and to gain a good feel for a company's culture before applying for a job. While social media such as Facebook and Instagram can be used for spreading the word, like "I'm looking for a job in marketing," LinkedIn is the ultimate job-seeker's tool. It's where to spend most of the limited digital time that you have. You don't have the time to do everything, so do this.

Prepare to share samples of your work

If you are in an artistic field or have past work experience that is visual, you must be prepared to share samples of your work both on your personal website and in person.

In some fields you will be expected to share your portfolio, which can include work that you created in school. You may be asked to submit this online. Be ready for this by preparing digital files of your work in advance or by creating a personal website that displays your work. If you are in the arts or a design field this is standard, and you can submit links in advance. When submitting your resume and cover letter online, be sure to include live links to your online work or website.

A personal website can bring your work alive to a prospective employer. It's not essential, so don't let the lack of a website slow you down in your job search. If you are going to create a personal website, find some websites you like and model yours after them. Keep it simple. Make it easy for an employer to find your resume, see your work and know how to contact you. Remember, you are just starting out and no one is going to compare your site to that of someone who has a long career in your field.

Show your best work first

When you are there in person and asked to show samples of your work, always show your best work first. Don't save it for last or for a big build-up! Your interviewer may have limited time, so make sure that they'll remember the big first impression. Use this formula whenever you are making a presentation...start with the best. Follow it with the second best. Put lesser work in the middle. Close your presentation with the third best.

Once you get the job, remember this as you present your work and ideas to others. Best is always first.

Bring your portfolio when showing art or design, even if it's available online

Bring your portfolio to your interview, even if it is digitized and you have sent links to the interviewer. Who knows whether the interview room will have a computer or a connection? Do not drop off your work in advance unless you are asked to do so. Portfolios of your work are excellent tools to stimulate conversation. However, most companies do not want to be responsible for your originals or samples of your work before or after an interview, nor do they want to pay the postage or freight to return them.

Get a notebook holder, "padfolio" or small portfolio

There's no need to invest a lot in this, but you will need a professional-looking way to bring your resume and cover letter to a live interview. Always bring at least three copies with you, even if you already submitted these items online. You never know exactly who might be in attendance, even though you've asked in advance! You may also use your padfolio to bring in notes that you've made and questions you want to ask. You'll want to be equipped with a pen and notepad so that you can make notes during the interview. Asking for these at the site makes you look unprepared.

Also, don't assume that the interviewer will have your resume in-hand because sometimes they won't. Likely they're in the middle of a busy workday and if you are prepared and deliver a fresh copy of your resume, it might just make your interview the most successful one of the day. Arrive with what you need to show, even if it's a print-out.

Everyone who works with me knows that I always "bring one for Elvis." My team sets an extra place, brings an extra meeting agenda and shows up with at least one extra copy of whatever for someone we didn't expect. Elvis" may be the person who hires you.

Look right for the job

If you are applying for a job as a banker, look like a banker. If you are applying for work in rock and roll or for a maverick tech company, then your Billie Eilish hair may be a hit, as long as it feels right to you.

How hip do you want to look? It depends on the job. But keep this in mind: If you have to edit who you are to apply for a job, perhaps you are applying for the wrong job. That's different than stepping up your look to apply for a job... it's trying to change who you are to fit into a job.

Also, your region of the country makes a difference in the relative fashions of the day for the work world. For example, despite the fact that they're all located on the coast in California, attire norms vary dramatically between San Diego, Newport Beach, Los Angeles and San Francisco. Get in synch with where you are interviewing.

Some industries are more informal than others, and some people are naturally hipper. I worked in advertising (sort of hip but not really) and then fine arts (where people expect you to express yourself via your attire). Use your judgement!

Be intentional with your interviewing wardrobe

You can start with two outfits or one suit and keep going. The trick is to have coordinates that work together and simple touches to create different looks.

For a business professional career like banker, attorney or upper-level professional, a fitted suit is the best business accessory you can have. Find one that:

- Can be worn in most seasons (think black or blue plus a color)
- Packs easily and does not wrinkle
- Includes pieces that can work together to create multiple looks

Consider dressing in layers so that you can dress up or down depending on the environment or the wardrobes of your interview team, whether online or in person. If you're too dressy, you can take off your jacket and be more casual.

Media executive Lynda Keeler recommends that when interviewing, keep a scarf in your purse. If you need to be dressier, put it on, and if you spill coffee on your shirt, you can cover it.

Now you have all the tools! It's time to interview!

Chapter 4
Get Interviews for the Right Jobs for You

Find the right place to work. Show up as the real you.
Be prepared, because your first chance at an interview
is your best chance. If you are ready, you can nail it.

Use your contacts to get started

The best way to get an interview is via people you know connecting you with people that they know. And once you start the interviewing process, you will likely find that people close to you know a lot of people, or someone close to you is a "networker."

As you begin to interview, you may find yourself meeting with exactly the person who will take an interest in you and your career search. You may also find yourself meeting with a stranger that seemingly can't help you at all. The secret is not to judge. Throughout my career I have found that when someone welcomes me in, I am about to learn something valuable or make a contact that may matter for life. So say yes, even if the introduction seems a bit off track.

Always remember that when you are recommended for an interview, whoever set things in motion is betting on you to deliver. They expect that you'll show up on time, look right and make a good impression. They are sticking their neck out for you, so right after your interview, be sure to get back in touch and let them know how it went via a phone call or email. In addition, immediately email a thank you note to the person who interviewed you and place a handwritten note to the interviewer in the mail that day. That's right, do both. The handwritten note is an extra touch, like putting a gold star next to your name. Just do it! It makes a singular strong impression and could be the extra touch that gets you the job.

"Be persistent and consistent in everything you do," says Jennifer Slaughter. "Go after it in a methodical, thoughtful way."

Network to get interviews

Leverage your relationships...to network. Networking is a way of opening doors that open doors that open doors. Your career now and throughout your life will be about relationships. The best way to build relationships is to actually meet people in person. That's your goal.

The top-notch LinkedIn profile and optional personal website that we discussed in the last chapter are important here; you'll want to get these in place before you proceed. I also recommend that you buy a box of simple, gender-neutral, professional-looking thank you cards and invest in inexpensive business cards from a local quick printer or an online source. Give the business cards to everyone you meet, including casual acquaintances, and tell them you're looking for a job. Then send friends and acquaintances to your website and LinkedIn profile to learn all about you.

Let's talk about where to start networking:

- **Friends and family** – Start in the most comfortable circle and build outward from there. Who do they know? They can easily recommend you to their contacts. Most likely they are willing to help make introductions, put you up in a strange city and show you around, introduce you to their friends and help you get started. Tap this resource if you are looking for a job either locally or far away.

- **Friends of friends and family** – That's your next circle. It's still a warm circle because it is full of relationships and warm connections. Friends of friends really count. Don't be shy or reluctant to approach. When you ask, "Who do you know that would be willing to talk with me about a career in my field?" you may get some very big surprises. People love to talk about what they know. A simple phone call may get you in the door. After all, you are not asking for a job interview. You are asking for help in meeting people. Remember, actually meeting people in person or via Zoom is the key to success.

- **Acquaintances** – Making the effort to take conversations beyond sterile pleasantries will build lasting relationships and broaden your network. Don't be shy when you can really use some help here. When you tell your barista and hair stylist that you're looking, really connect with them about why you believe they'd be good at helping you and let them know what you are looking for in a career and why. One of the strongest ways to build a relationship with someone is to ask them to do a favor for you. It shows that you trust them. It's easy to say, "You know a lot of people. I am looking for a starting job in communications or public relations. If you can help me spread the word, I'd really appreciate it. Here are a couple of my business cards."

Reach acquaintances by putting the word out on social media as well. Who do you know? Many more people than you believe! And who do they know? Many, many more! Pick one or two social media outlets to use to round out your job search. You don't need more and won't have time for them, either.

- **College and alumni networks** – Loyalty to your alma mater runs deep! Tap this valuable resource of shared interests and connections to your college and even high school. The same is true with any clubs or special interest groups to which you have belonged. Were you a member of the intercollegiate chess club or rowing team? If they have a Facebook page, website or other means of communications, use that to get the word out.

- **People you meet by volunteering** – No, this is not a crazy thought. Of course, you are busy, possibly working while seeking a job or spending most of your time in the search. However, an excellent way to meet new people and build your network of contacts is to volunteer for a cause or organization that matches your interests. By working on a team with a shared goal, you are likely to meet a wide variety of new people, from "worker bees" to CEOs, while you are relaxing, having fun and doing something good for the world. If you have moved to a new community, volunteering is an excellent way to connect. Plus, it accomplishes that big purpose of meeting new contacts in person.

Even in the age of the Internet, the best way to get jobs is to meet people in person. Facetime, Skype, Zoom and other internet-based interviews are the next best thing. The interviewer will be watching you and you will be watching them. While not as good as meeting in the flesh, the online interview is still a powerful way to start a relationship.

Find real jobs that are available now

Become a searcher. You can find job postings in a variety of ways, including:

- **Via the big, general job posting sites** – Although these sites are loaded with opportunities, it's hard to stand out amongst the crush of applicants. I have yet to meet someone who landed a job from one, yet I know people who have spent hour after hour on these sites looking for their perfect job. Use the filters on these sites and have them push jobs to you, in order to avoid spending lots of unproductive time.
- **Via industry-specific sites** – These sites, which are often run by trade associations within an industry, enable you

to make a much more targeted search. Usually these sites list fresh jobs at all levels of the companies that are association members, from intern to CEO. Member companies like to use these sites to reach job candidates because only people looking for jobs in their industry visit the sites and apply. Association sites may or may not be open to non-members.

- **Via company websites** – Check to see if the employers that are of interest to you post jobs on their own websites. If so, this is an outstanding online starting place. Sometimes a company site will say that no jobs are currently open but encourage you to send a resume. If you have that organization in your sights, send your resume and a strong cover letter. Better yet, if you are looking for a job locally, stop by in person and drop off your resume. It's your first step to learning more about the company and building a relationship.
- **Newspapers** – Yes, good old-fashioned newspapers and their classifieds, both online and printed, remain a way to learn about jobs as soon as they open. Pay attention to your local news media and you may be the first among your friends to land a great job!

Be open to working your way up

Once I had the opportunity to hear the CEO of a major outdoor brand speak to a local Chamber of Commerce in a mountain community. The crowd was filled with athletes—strong bikers, skiers, hikers and adventurers. Of course, the first audience question was, "How do we get jobs with your company?" The CEO's response was immediate. "Get a job in one of our stores to get to know the company and its products and become a 'brand evangelist.'"

According to the CEO, knowing the company's values, products and operations from the inside was the best possible way in the door and up the corporate staircase for an organization like theirs that recognizes and promotes talent from within. It makes total sense.

Working retail may not sound like the best possible career move to your friends and parents, but if you are focused on a career in a particular retail industry niche, such as sports or fashion, and you mention to your interviewer that you want to learn more about the company because you have done your homework and would like a career with them, your interviewer's ears will perk up. If you are being sincere and honest, you may walk out with a job.

To your friends and parents, your retail job may not sound sexy, but you're earning money while learning, and you're possibly eligible for health insurance and other benefits while you apply for advancement opportunities along the way. Stores have growth paths into management training and are looking for exceptional recruits, and smart employers give preference to existing employees before talking to outsiders to fill their jobs.

Go in when you see that the tent flap is up!

Opportunities go to those who present themselves. Sometimes you may be in the right place with the right person to help you get on board in a specific industry, and no matter how shy you may be, you'll have to take the opportunity or lose it. It can be as simple as introducing yourself to the person, quickly mentioning your interest in their field and asking if they would be open to receiving your resume. When you have the opportunity, take it.

For example, years ago I read in the newspaper that the Nevada state photographer was leaving. Having worked on the Governor's campaign as a photographer, I caught the Governor as he was entering his office to ask about it. Although the job had been eliminated, he asked for my resume. I joined his staff as Administrative Assistant.

If you have a business card, share it. If not, find out the best way to reach the person with whom you just spoke. Respect their time and thank them. Make sure that your first impression is organized and business-like, the opposite of an "ambush." Then see where it goes. Life just dealt you a possibility, so take it!

Use a great tool: The informational interview

You may be thinking that you'd like a certain career, but don't really know enough about it to make a good choice. How can you find out more? A respected tool is the informational interview. If you have an interest in a particular field, it's okay to contact someone who is working at a junior or senior level in that field and ask if you can meet with them for an informational interview. You'll be regarded as eager and sincere and will gain access to someone who may be able to truly help you in your career.

Jennifer Slaughter, Chief Marketing Officer for a large hospital, says "yes" to these requests because she believes in helping young people get ahead in their careers (that's important!). She has her own agenda here, too, because she uses these opportunities to evaluate potential job candidates. Granting informational interviews allows Jennifer to keep her finger on the pulse of the job market while helping a prospective job candidate at the same time.

On her way up in her own career, Jennifer used informational interviews to get her foot in the door to build relationships that later resulted in real jobs. For example, while reading a regional business magazine she saw that an executive who had granted her an informational interview three years prior had received a promotion. She wrote a note of congratulations to the woman and was invited for an interview that resulted in a job offer.

When Jennifer knew that in 12 months she'd be moving from Minnesota to Colorado, she prepared for a visit by asking a marketing firm there for an informational interview. When it was time for the move she re-contacted the Colorado company. Her resume went to the top of the heap and she was hired on arrival.

JENNIFER SLAUGHTER

Jennifer created a career that has built upon itself.

When I interviewed Jennifer for this book, she was waiting for the first case of coronavirus to be diagnosed in the Roaring Fork Valley in Colorado. As Chief of Marketing for Aspen Valley Hospital, she was on full alert and her team was ready. As usual, she was prepared and ready for whatever would be coming at her.

Jennifer was in a meeting with our marketing team when I first met her. Her eyes were bright with the discussion of the future of our non-profit arts center, Anderson Ranch in Aspen/Snowmass, Colorado. Combined with her energy and enthusiasm, Jennifer's ethic and aptitude for hard work made her a standout among consultants. When the job of marketing director at the Ranch opened up, she was the only person I called.

Out of her comfort zone by creating her own company, Jennifer knew she could rely on herself—and that's a trait we needed in the person who would run our communications and grow our non-profit's reputation. Jennifer has had her dream job many times. She is not bound by one concept of herself and her capabilities.

For example, when she was just out of college Jennifer started with a paid internship in the international division of a Minneapolis advertising agency. Though friends and family had questioned her choice of the German language as one of her college majors, it was the nudge that opened more than one career door for her. After a summer of interning, she got her second dream job with a renowned branding agency. Within two weeks she was on an international flight to Germany, meeting with clients there. Jennifer spent three years in that job and then moved to another job with a market research firm. Throughout, she regularly lined up "informational interviews" with companies where she believed she'd like to work.

Having met a man from Minneapolis who'd moved West, Jennifer eventually left her uptown apartment in Minneapolis to begin a new career with a small marketing firm in a rural Colorado community. An informational interview opened the door. Every time she had visited her fiancé in Colorado, she had arranged for at least one informational interview. When an opening occurred, her resume was at the top of the pile for an account executive...who spoke German.

Among the many projects we tackled together at Anderson Ranch were creating a long-range plan and a 50-year anniversary program and companion book. Jennifer's ability to clearly communicate complex information and keep a team of staff and Board members moving forward and informed on very complicated projects is unparalleled.

Jennifer understands the importance of working for organizations that share her values. Once she had an interview with a company that just felt wrong. "The interviewer kept repeating the same question, as if to get me to change my answer," she recalls. "It felt really heavy. Afterwards, I felt like a failure. I did not get the job." But later she realized that it wasn't the right place for her anyway and quit trying for big corporate jobs. "I went for things that were a bit lighter, more entrepreneurial in spirit," she says with a smile.

For Jennifer, success is in making a positive impact. "I have to know I'm making a difference," she declares. Anyone who is lucky enough to work with Jennifer knows she does this every day.

Once the word is out to your friends and family that you are looking for a job, they may have some great ideas and contacts for you for informational interviews. "Who do you know that...?" is a great question. When they have prospective contacts for you, ask them to open the door with an introductory email or phone call to their contact so that you can follow up and set an appointment. They can copy you on the introductory email and you can introduce yourself from there.

If you don't know the person you'd like to meet and have no obvious way in the door, a short email (three sentences or so) can be helpful. Remember, you are approaching a busy person. For example:

Ms. Watkins,

You are involved in a dynamic industry that offers exciting career opportunities. I recently graduated from Center Community College with a degree in finance and would appreciate the opportunity to meet you for an informational interview to learn more about your company and experiences. I sincerely appreciate your interest and time.

Thank you in advance for your consideration.

Tanisha Evers

Keep in mind that informational interviews are just that. Informational. They are not job interviews unless the person you have contacted happens to be looking for an employee.

Often the person you contacted will send you down the ladder to someone who reports to them. Don't be disappointed. Be elated! You're getting an interview and that's a great start.

Likely you will meet your host in their workplace, giving you the opportunity to see how it operates, meet co-workers and experience how they respond to you and their work world. Informational interviews provide golden opportunities to envision yourself in a career.

Does the company website show the team members? How are they dressed? Can you match their attire and look like you are a fit for the company? While an informational interview is not a job interview, it may become one, so prepare for it as if it could be.

Ask probing questions in your informational interview

Before showing up, be sure to put together an excellent list of questions. Do your homework. Go online to learn all that you can about the career, the company and the person you are meeting. Is your host's bio posted in the staff section of the website? Study it well so that when you go in, you can ask questions that will show that you have researched the company and the industry and that you value the host's time.

Here are some questions to put on your list:
- What drew you to this industry?
- How did you get started in your career in this industry?
- What is your typical day?
- What are your favorite things about your work and career?

- What skills are needed to be successful in this industry?
- Where is the industry growing? Where is it shrinking?
- What would you change if you could?
- If you were me, where would you start on a new career in this field?
- What is one piece of advice that would be valuable to know in seeking a job in your field?

You have a very important thing in your hands: access to real information. Be prepared to make the most of it!

Consider a job if it connects with your passion

Mary Ackermann Gaer loves the process of construction and the finished product. Her enthusiasm enabled her to talk easily with prospective employers as she started on her path to becoming a licensed general contractor. But initially, she was hired as a receptionist for a company that did not take women seriously. They didn't hire her for her experience in accounts payable. They hired her because she was cute.

Mary knew it, but stayed in that job until she learned all she could about running a construction office, including bookkeeping, payroll and hiring, and acquired the skills she needed to go further. Then she stepped out on her own, building a career in construction that, at the time, would defy all odds—a woman commanding a large housing construction site. First, though, she got in the door that connected with her passion and learned all she could.

Sometimes the first job seems so unimportant, but often it's just the entrée to a huge career. After all, you are on a journey and this could be the first step on the road. If you are connecting your interests with opportunities, you are on the right road.

Explore whether you wish to intern

If you choose to intern, be sure that you are working in an area where you can learn skills to advance into the directions you desire. Some internships are paid and some are not. Before taking an internship, get a good gauge of the opportunity and the company's hiring record with interns. I know one bright young woman who interned for a professional firm in a very expensive market for a year but did not get a job offer. In the interim, they used her and used her up.

Not everyone can afford either unpaid or paid internships. Your situation will dictate your choices. If you choose to intern, do your homework in advance to make sure that you are entering into a valuable experience that you can leverage for your future.

Chapter 5
Interview Like a Pro

Be authentic, be yourself and be well-prepared. You will feel comfortable throughout the interview process and create a connection with your interviewer that makes you memorable.

Be ready to share the benefits of the work you have already done

Colby Fisher Dailey stepped off the elevator into a world of marble and glass for her first interview on the 50th floor of the Bank of America building. She had left small town Fraser, Colorado (pop. 1,300) for Los Angeles shortly after college and a short stint of working with my husband and me in our marketing and PR firm.

Colby wanted to go where she could be on the beach and learn how to surf. But, as she says, "I was too responsible to leave without a plan." So she had connected in advance with a temp agency. The job for which she was interviewing was in the office services department of a financial giant, supporting the company's corporate team. Colby told them of her work at a 5-star guest ranch where extreme hospitality service was the norm. To show how her work experiences would apply to their job she shared an example of a demanding guest who wanted fresh towels at 6:00 am daily, and how she delivered.

Colby entered this company's impressive corporate hallways, which were decorated with original Ansel Adams photographs, wearing her "interview suit" and her smile. She got the job and started on a career path to working in social justice.

"I had no financial qualifications in my background, but I saw that if I was able to fill a niche with a corporate foundation, I could find my place there and gain a toehold toward doing the work I do now." In charge of the company's philanthropic gifts program just four years later, Colby was able to make a real difference for people and non-profits during her seven years with the company.

But that day she was just Colby, fresh in from Colorado interviewing to get a starter job.

What Colby brought to that interview was sincerity and the courage to be her true self. She did not twist herself into what they wanted to see. Instead, she listened to their needs, reviewed her skills and experience and applied them to the questions she was asked.

COLBY FISHER DAILEY

Colby's worldview has always been bigger than the small town where she was born; her opportunities would come from somewhere else.

Colby Fisher Dailey is a small-town girl with a big career. Growing up in Fraser, Colorado was not a limiting factor in her universe. Instead, it was a grounding factor for a young woman who would launch like a rocket.

Following college Colby worked briefly for us in our marketing business. It was immediately evident in the way she handled herself that she was going to create some big opportunities. Colby is my niece, and I include her here because I am proud to share her success.

Early in her life Colby knew that she had the benefit of growing up in a positive environment. She had supportive parents, was able to go to good schools and, during her summers, work in a high-quality resort. Colby decided to place herself on a career path that would address social injustice. "I saw that some doors were open to me but not to others," she said. But she needed experience.

After leaving our marketing business Colby got a job in the global financial world. It was here that she got her toehold into a company with a large foundation. Colby turned that toehold into a footprint as she spent five years working her way toward the philanthropic area of the foundation, where all of the grantmaking and organizational funding decisions were made.

Her hard work paid off when she was promoted to the position of Senior Program Officer. In this role Colby learned how to navigate in the C-suite, working with the CEO and executive leadership team in a job that called for decorum, sensitivity and vision. Colby loved the job and stayed for two years, until working with an uncollaborative co-worker prompted her to reevaluate her career and take her next steps.

"I realized that organizations could do more and that I could do more," she said. Colby went on to obtain a graduate degree in public policy at UC Berkeley and help organizations obtain capital in order to advance their missions. "I felt that organizations' philanthropic investments could have more impact through partnerships and new community investment models," she explains.

Colby became the senior advisor for a national center she co-founded that pairs community development and healthcare. They build teams of funders to invest in low-income communities, continuing her work with big-name partners, foundations including Ford and Rockefeller. The goal: Help change the lives of people in America who do not have access to good housing and health care. "We are focused on impact investing," she says, proud to be making a difference by building programs in communities all over the U.S. for people who need help. "The roots of poverty and poor health are the same."

Dedicated to growing her own leadership abilities, Colby advises young women to "really articulate your personal and professional values and lead with those." Colby also believes in the value of investing to grow your leadership abilities.

"My worldview was always bigger than Fraser," she says. She knows that she was fortunate to have had a good education, a supportive family and some opportunities that had opened early to her. She has built a career using those gifts to help others.

Show up on time and in the right frame of mind

Here is my "tried and true" advice, a 24-hour schedule to prevent panic for the in-person interview, and many steps that apply to the online interview, as well.

- **Give yourself more time than you need** for every step so that it is not possible that you will be late.

- **Plan your wardrobe to the last detail the day before**, and then put it all on to make sure that you have everything you need and it all fits well and looks good. Then take it all off, put it together in the closet and on the dresser until you need it. Place all of your accessories in one bag and keep it with your clothes (hang the bag on a hanger). Don't forget shoes.

- **Load your briefcase or notepad holder the day before**. Don't wait till the last minute in case you need an extra copy of your resume or cover letter. This is about avoiding panic. Remember....your printer will never work when you need it in a hurry! You will look more professional with just one bag, so take essentials from your purse and find a place for them in your briefcase, instead. You don't need much—lipstick, glasses, driver's license, keys, money, subway or bus pass, a comb or mini-brush and small mirror will get you through.

- **If practical, do a test visit to the interview location the day before** to scout traffic delays, parking and any things you might encounter that would make you late the day of. If you are taking the bus or subway, do a test run and get the timing from your doorway to theirs.

- **Get a good night's sleep the night before.** This is one evening you do not have to go out with the girls or watch late night shows.

- **On the day of, get up and go,** and arrive 15 minutes early for your interview.

- **To avoid jitters while waiting,** stand up and look around the office. It will give you good clues as to what the company and/or your interviewer do. Many companies put their "stuff" in the lobby. You'll get some insights here. Is Popular Mechanics from 2001 on the waiting room table or are Forbes or Architectural Digest from this month proudly positioned there? Remember, you're looking for clues.

- **Ask the receptionist how to pronounce the interviewer's name.** If you are unsure of this, now is an excellent time to get clarification. Repeat it to yourself a few times so you will remember.

- **If you can, greet your interviewer while standing.** Don't sit down. Cruise around. Start out on an equal level. Look your interviewer in the eye as you greet them by name, "Hi, Phuong. It's a pleasure to meet you."

- **Silence your cell phone and put it away.** Go cold turkey until you get out of there. I mean way out of there...off of their turf entirely! You never know who is listening.

- **Go for it.** Good job! You started out calm and collected and you can do it! Know that you can nail this interview.

Observe your surroundings

Whether you are interviewing online or in person, you'll quickly pick up the essence of the company. Online you can't tell if the furniture in the office is fancy, but you can tell if they have class. Are you meeting with the person you anticipated or are they too busy and do you feel passed off? Are they upbeat and positive? Do you experience a sense of their pride in their work and their company? Are they excited about what they are doing, and do they convey a sense of excitement about having a new person like you join their team? You can pick up a lot of clues in the early stages of connecting.

One CEO I especially liked came directly into the lobby to greet me. He did not send his executive assistant but invited her to join us in our session in case follow-up work was needed. His style was warm and friendly, as was the entire workplace.

One young woman had two offers at once. The company she believed she wanted to join reached out to her once following the interview and offer while the other company contacted her thirteen times with news, updates and information. "They really wanted me," she said, and that's where she went.

Consider the interviewer

Interviewing is like a dance. It takes at least two, and you are interviewing them as they are interviewing you. Of course, as you prep for an interview, you're thinking, "It's all about me." But maybe it isn't. Consider the mindset of the interviewer. They've got a problem to solve. Either the company is growing and needs more good people, or something has happened to create a vacancy. When you walk or Zoom into their universe, do your best to show that you are the right person for the job and the right fit for the company based upon the research that you've done.

Hiring the wrong person is an absolute disaster for any company. It's possible that your interviewer's job could be on the line with this hire so they may be as nervous as you are. They're thinking, "How will this young woman contribute to our firm? Will she stay or quickly jump ship? Will she willingly tackle her assignments and take on more? Will we get a good return from our investment in her? Is she the one? Or will she be filing for unemployment in three months because she wasn't a good fit and we had to let her go?"

Stand out by connecting with the interviewer

Business owner Tiana Webb Evans believes it's crucial to establish yourself in the first thirty seconds of a conversation. "They always say you have only one chance to make a first impression. Are you creating an opportunity for connection?" She encourages interviewees to be memorable when they meet potential employers and quickly figure out how they can add value.

"Create a connection with your interviewer," agrees media VP Lynda Keeler. "Be memorable."

In researching the company and the interviewer to create your Job Interview Worksheet, you have Googled the interviewer to find out more about them, including information that can be used to create a connection. Perhaps you found out that the interviewer is a film buff, and you are, too. That's valuable to know.

"Try to fit your skills into what they are looking for," says realtor Mary Ackermann Gaer, "both during your interview and on paper, meaning in your cover letter and in your follow-up."

In your research you've been fearless, searching all of the popular social media sites looking for information that may help you create some shared ground for conversation. If you don't find any pearls, some may come up when you talk. When you create a connection with your interviewer, you are pulling yourself forward in the interview process and accomplishing a very important goal...making yourself memorable.

Present yourself with purpose. Address your interviewers by looking directly at them. Don't be rushed or in a hurry. The interviewer has set aside time for you and you have spent your time preparing. Be relaxed because you are prepared.

Let your interviewer know that you've done your homework

You've done a good job researching the company and the opportunity. Now let your interviewer know.

For example, let's say you do your background research for a job as marketing assistant and discover that the company with which you are interviewing has an office in Paris. During your interview you mention that you know they have a Paris office with a marketing component, and you speak French. You'll deliver the best single impression that you could have made: She did her homework.

Ask lots of questions when interviewing for a job. People love to talk about what they know.

Smile and be authentic

In an interview, you can smile and show your sense of humor. It will make you stand out. Authenticity is a common trait I have found amongst the successful women I've known. They don't manufacture answers to suck up to others, including interviewers. They answer in a straightforward manner, telling their truths.

"What's your eventual goal?" I was asked when interviewing for my starter job with the ad agency. "I'd like to run a big ranch," I answered honestly while seated in their office in Milwaukee. That goal was going to take a lot of work and many years and had nothing to do with advertising, but it's what I wanted. And they saw it. I had real goals. And they hired me.

Know that it's okay to ask questions

Is it a new job? What was the reason behind creating it? Or was it an existing job? Perhaps someone left or perhaps a problem or situation that may be valuable to know about happened to cause the vacancy. You can ask, and asking will help you gain insight into where you may be headed if take this job.

Also be sure to ask, "What will my typical day look like?" This question will really help you understand the nature of the work you will be doing.

Expect to hear, "Tell me about yourself"

Repeatedly in your job search you will be asked, "Tell me about yourself." In fact, it's often the first question of the interview. Colby Fisher Dailey says, "Learn how to tell your own story. Talk about why and how you do what you do. Find a way to plainly articulate your personal and professional values and lead with those."

"I'm focused on a career in veterinary medicine because I value all life and believe that animals deserve excellent care," would be an example when discussing why you want to work at the National Zoo. Go on from there as you talk briefly about yourself and what you will bring to this new opportunity.

Be practiced but casual and keep it short. Practice, practice, practice telling your story so that you can easily say it without it sounding forced or stiff. For a job interview, a 90-second story will likely suffice, enabling you to deliver important information without overdoing it.

Be ready for questions like these

Some interviewers ask big, loopy questions like, "What is your goal in life?"

Also expect to have very direct questions like, "What do you know about our company?" and "Why do you believe you'd be a good fit in this job?" Because you have done deep homework before you walked in the door for the interview, you know all about the company, what they do and what their mission is.and you have taken the time to think through why you'd belong there. You're ready for these important questions!

Expect the interviewer to zero in on your experience. They are looking for the essence of you, so it's okay to have a sense of humor and smile.

Some interviewers ask trick-type questions. I was in one where the candidate was asked, "What is the dumbest thing you have ever done?" We did not hire the candidate that told us that it was taking her boyfriend on her dream trip to Europe... which he ruined for her. As she was still with him, this example showed us that she lacked strong problem-solving skills.

What's the smartest thing you've done or an example of something of which you're extremely proud? Be ready with an example of something you've done that made a difference. It does not necessarily need to be about work.

"Where do you see yourself in ten years?" I asked this of a job candidate for an entry position in finance and she had a very direct answer: "I'll own five rental houses by then." Wow. She was good. But not everyone knows their answer. If you have a vision for yourself and your career, be ready to share it. If not, don't be hard on yourself. This may be your first job and crucial to forming that vision. You're just starting your career.

I did not know that I wanted to run an ad agency until after I worked at one, but I did believe I'd enjoy a job where I could use my creativity and learn the ad business. Andy Sachs in "The Devil Wore Prada" didn't know she wanted to be a writer until she side-tracked into working for a fashion icon. Be honest with yourself and your interviewer and you'll make the right impression.

Be open to taking a test or solving a problem

For some jobs, you may be asked to take a test or perform a task. If you are being hired for a particular expertise, the employer may want proof. Don't be offended.

I hired an assistant who did not know the difference between "it's" and "its." Consequently, every business letter and grant proposal required extensive proofing to find the grammatical errors and fix them. I learned my lesson. Thereafter, I asked candidates to write samples so that I could see their true command of the English language.

Sometimes these tests involve potential "gotchas" that you might not see coming. For example, one recent engineering graduate was flown to Apple's headquarters in Cupertino, California for a long day of interviews. As part of the process she was given time to solve an engineering problem, after which she had to present her solution. When she explained that she designed the solution specifically to use a standard, off-the-shelf screw in order to save money, their facial expressions showed she'd made an error. Although she thought she had done her homework, the response blindsided her. "We're Apple. We do not use off-the-shelf parts. Even our screws are custom-made."

Be ready for anything

Be ready for anything and know that if you have completed your Personal Inventory, Job Interview Worksheet and Personal Career Map, you will be far ahead of many other candidates. Both your questions and your answers will show the interviewer that you are secure in yourself and knowledgeable about the company and the opportunity.

Sometimes you'll be interviewed by one person and sometimes by an entire department. Be sure to write down the names of all your interviewers and keep them in front of you. That way you can address them by name if there is a group. Also, you'll be able to send a thank you note that mentions the team members by name, showing that you cared and paid attention.

Suzy Welch, columnist, journalist and best-selling author, posted a video on LinkedIn about the candidate who landed the job as her assistant. After an excellent interview Suzy thought she'd selected her person, even though the interviewee didn't seem to know much about the job. But the next candidate blew her away. This candidate had all of the qualifications and experience Suzy sought, and she had driven to the work site the evening prior to make sure that she knew where to go, where to park and how to be on time. That degree of preparation caught Suzy's attention—and guess who became her assistant.

Recognize that interviewing online requires special preparation

In today's world, it's as likely that you will be interviewed online as in person. To prepare, you'll need to do a few practice runs with a friend or sibling on the software that will be used. Also, you'll want to be dressed in the practice runs just like you will appear in the interview, including wardrobe, hair and make-up.

Smoothly using the videoconferencing software is vitally important. If you waste the first five to 15 minutes of your precious interview fumbling around trying to figure it out (or, worse, trying to login), you may be disqualified before you even have a chance to speak. Practice makes perfect. Be sure you have downloaded the latest version of the software (if necessary) and are confident in your ability to use it.

Regardless of which videoconferencing software will be used, a simple, uncluttered background will be very important. Find the right place, and if all you have to work with is a bedroom, find an angle that does not include your bed. Adjust the light to be sure that your face is softly lit and not dark. Be sure to check the lighting at various times of day—both the hour at which your interview is scheduled, and other times in case it is moved at the last minute. If you find that you are doing a lot of online interviews, you may want to invest in a ring light that attaches to your monitor for better lighting. Ask your practice partner to be critical. If you can, tape the interview to evaluate and improve your performance.

Plan to dress for the interview from head to toe and appear just as though you are headed into their office doorway for an actual sit-down. Don't cheat on this, as you may need to get up and retrieve a paper and don't want to reveal that you're in shorts. Your online wardrobe can consist of basic darks. Jewelry will look nice on the dark background, and earrings will reflect the sparkle in your eyes. If you are interviewing for a formal job where you would normally wear a suit for an interview, then wear a suit for your online interview! Be who you want them to hire, and don't dress down because the interview feels more casual since it's in your home.

Makeup and lipstick keep you from looking washed out on screen. If you have any questions about this, watch network TV anchors to see how they look.

Place your computer on something elevated, such as a couple of thick books, to bring it up to eye level so that you are not looking down. Look at the camera, which is just like looking your interviewer directly in the eye. Look forward and directly ahead.

Keep your resume and cover letter for this company together in a separate file on your desktop so that you can quickly access and send them if someone unexpectedly enters the "online room."

As part of the interview, it's okay to ask about expectations for working from home vs. working at the office.

Close the interview

Whether you are meeting in person or online, as you close the interview, ask about the hiring process, particularly what the next steps are and when they hope to make a decision.

Chapter 6
Get the Offer and Salary You Want

Be prepared to close the deal to your satisfaction.

Have a sense of what the job will pay before you interview

One of the most nerve-wracking parts of the interview process is the offer and salary negotiation. Questions about your salary expectations can come up on the first or second interview. Be ready to answer when the interviewer asks, "What sort of salary are you looking for?" They are trying to determine whether or not they can afford you. They have a salary in mind. In some cases they may also be trying to determine if they can get you for "below budget." You can respond by asking the pay range of the job, or you can respond by stating the range you are looking for.

After all, you should have a salary in mind, too. You must know what you expect to be paid. Do your homework before the interview by going online to find out typical salaries for similar jobs in your part of the country. Let them know that you came prepared. "I researched Ultrasound Technician jobs in the Midwest, and found that starting salaries are in the range of $X to $Y."

Offering a range with the lowest salary you will accept at the bottom is always a good way to go. Let's say you would like to make $50,000 and your research shows that's a common starting salary for this job in this industry in this region. You can say, "$50,000 to $60,000." If they start you at the lowest rung, you're getting a fine salary with room to grow, and based upon your research, you're already off to a great start. Respect yourself and you will earn respectable pay.

By law in some states, a prospective employer cannot ask what you made in your last job. They can ask if you have any "salary requirements," meaning "what are you expecting to make?" It's never comfortable at this point, but if you are prepared with information and data you'll be fine.

Nail the second interview

If you are asked back for a second interview, what does that mean? It means that you're in the running and they want to go a bit deeper with you. You may be one of several candidates asked back, so you don't have the job yet, but your chances are much better.

To prepare, go over all of your notes from the first interview to formulate really insightful questions about the role and the responsibilities it entails. How does your role fit with the mission of the company? Showing an understanding of the company, its products or services and customers will really make you stand out in this interview. Spend your time here on substance. Envision yourself in this job and think about some of the challenges you may have or problems you may be asked to solve and how your skills will guide you easily through. Take a walk and start to dream. Give yourself space to think. Fill your mind with scenarios. You're getting ready to get this.

During the second visit, you may be interviewed by a team of people who would become your co-workers. This would give you an excellent opportunity to get a feeling for the organization. Is it friendly, funny, super serious? Perhaps you'll be taken on a facilities tour. Whatever the job, be sure to dress so that you can go where your prospective employer may take you. On one interview, I was escorted through 44 acres of heavy industry. Fortunately, I'd anticipated a tour and had worn flats.

Expect to have these conversations that may come up now or with an offer

To whom will you report? Have you met that person? Be sure that you do before accepting a job. Can you meet the team with whom you'll work?

You will want to know about salary and benefits. What is the salary? When would you start? Is health insurance included? How many vacation days are offered and when can they be taken? What about sick days?

If you have a young child to take care of, you'll want to know if they offer any benefits such as childcare. Also, how does the company respond to your parental needs, like taking your kid(s) to the dentist or attending the school play during work hours?

Then you will want to know about how your performance will be evaluated and by whom and when, and if there is an opportunity for feedback, raises and promotions. Feedback enables you to move smarter and faster and understand what success looks like in your job.

Be ready when you get an offer

By now you've been through at least two rounds of interviews. You've had a tour of the offices or the campus (or you had an online gathering) and you've met a few people.

Just know that this can go either way. You may get a bomb of an offer but the chance to get onboard and grow. Or you may get everything you want and more. Either way, it's fine for you to say, "May I think about this and get back to you tomorrow?" or "I'd like to discuss this with my partner. Can I get back to you tomorrow?"

Whether you're initially delighted or disappointed, be delighted. You just broke through. You did your homework and sailed through your interviews and came out with a big win! I personally admit to accepting my first two job offers on the spot.

A fine line exists between knowing what you are worth and being paid what you are worth. Don't settle for less pay or benefits than you deserve. Be prepared to negotiate for something. If the salary offer is low, you may choose to negotiate for a higher wage or for being able to depart early one day a week or to do something that really matters to you. You can think this through and come back with it in responding to their offer. Be prepared, as you will only get one chance to accept, decline or negotiate.

If the offer is disappointing in terms of pay, is it a plus in terms of getting you into the industry you want or providing needed health insurance? Slice and dice it from all sides. Is this a company you really want to be part of, where you can see that a hand is pulling you into the circle? It's not all about money. Spend the time to make a good choice. And remember...this is a starter, early-career job. Your goal is to get started on the right path. Does this do that? It won't be forever. Will you learn new skills to take you to the next step?

You can ask if there is a chance for a review and a raise if you are doing well at the 90-day or six-month mark. By then you will know how good the job feels to you and they'll know if you are just getting by or doing really great work.

When you put things in context, you frame your decision. Ask these simple questions: "What's the best thing that can happen? What's the worst thing that can happen?" And then smile. You got this.

Be open to an offer for part-time work

Working part-time for a company is an outstanding way to get in the door and check them out. Understand that the minute you go to work for a company, they are investing in you. If you are a good performer, they'll be closely watching because it's not effective to have a company's investments walk out the door. People are a well-run company's biggest assets. If you have a chance to work part-time in an organization that's a desirable target for you, you can take it and perform to the max. You're in the door. If you like it, you are in a very good position to stay and grow with the company.

Get it in writing

Little is more comforting than to have the terms of your employment in writing, even in the simplest terms. Before you accept an offer, ask if you may have the terms of your employment in writing. Tell them that you'd like to be very clear about your agreement with them.

Why is it important to get your terms of employment in writing? Because things change. People change. Bosses leave or get promoted and one day you may arrive at work to find that you are working for a stranger who knows nothing about you or any details or terms of your employment. With your employment agreement letter, you have clarity about your job terms and responsibilities, and you have it in writing.

Your letter or employment agreement should include:
- Date of hire
- Job title
- Job description and duties
- Salary
- When salary is paid
- Commissions and terms to achieve them (for sales jobs)
- Bonus if offered and terms to achieve it
- That they will pay all payroll taxes as required by the state and federal governments
- Benefits offered to you (health insurance, dental, vision, 401k plan, more)
- Vacation time – amount, how it's accumulated and when you may take it
- Any other items that you have discussed and agreed upon that belong in writing

This need not be a legal document and can be a simple letter of agreement with both parties signing at the bottom...your signature as well as that of a qualified representative of theirs. Both parties must sign it for the agreement to be recognized. You may want to have your attorney or an experienced friend or family member review the agreement. If presented to you at work, it's okay to ask if you can take it home to review.

Your new employer may or may not have an Employee Handbook. If they do, you'll want to read it to be certain that this company and its policies align with your values. If they are a small business and have no handbook, that's okay. You may be in a position to help them create one.

Get started on your path

Tiana Webb Evans grew an entire career step-by-step by getting a foot in the door. Since landing her first job, Tiana has never applied for another. Growing up around business and working for her mom's travel agency since age five, Tiana knew how to dress, how to show up, how to work hard, how to be kind to everyone. She also knew the importance of learning how to do what no one else in the office wants to do, the piece that makes you invaluable.

Opportunity veered Tiana off of her "prescribed path" of a science-based career. Tiana's very first job was an internship at a design firm, not a biotech laboratory, because she simply needed a job to pay the rent. It wasn't what she'd expected from her graduate studies at NYU in science. "Many children of Caribbean descent are expected to be doctors, lawyers or engineers...that's the path. Art and design were hobbies, but not viewed as career paths," she says. Her idea was that she was going to be a doctor who owned an art gallery, not an odd phenomenon in Caribbean culture where professionals often own restaurants, hotels and clubs, living two career lives.

When in graduate school, a classmate mentioned that her cousin, who worked at a fancy design firm, was looking for an intern. At $15 an hour in 1997, it seemed like an excellent opportunity and Tiana pursued it. "I had wanted to be an art dealer and gallery owner ever since I was 13 years old. This was serendipity...I was fortunate to end up in a situation where I could see how I could actually make a decent living in the world I loved the most," she said. "On a very practical note, I was actually making a very sane decision. I was eventually offered a position making a salary that in my original career path would have taken me a Ph.D. and another $100,000 in tuition to secure."

At work, Tiana made friends with the firm's bookkeeper, who revealed that she was leaving to join a commune in California and offered to train Tiana to move into her job. When the bookkeeper resigned, she told management that they already had a replacement in Tiana. "I trained her." So, intern Tiana settled into the $35,000 per year salaried job, making a lot of money for a 24-year-old in 1998.

Tiana became friends with the business manager, who came to rely upon her for important tasks. Then she learned that the firm was replacing him. "How gutsy was I?" she asks, revealing that she wrote a proposal for the principal, who responded by calling her into his office. "I've never been afraid of talent and giving people a chance," he said. The job was hers.

At age 25, Tiana became the business manager of the 50-person firm responsible for the store design of major luxury brands like Gucci. Contracts, human resources, the bottom line...it was all, gladly, her problem. All because she mentioned to a classmate that she was looking for a job. Tiana went on to eventually build a highly-respected New York public relations firm that she runs today.

"Life is about relationships, who you know and who knows you," she says. "Are you making relationships that are meant to last a lifetime? There are no disposable business relationships. From the doorman to the CEO, everyone matters because you never know where you will meet again." It's been the story of her success.

TIANA WEBB EVANS

Tiana got one foot in the door that led step-by-step to a big career.

I first met Tiana as she was welcoming VIPs to an art event in Aspen for a high-profile client of hers. She is founder and CEO of ESP Group, LLC, New York, representing large art fairs, galleries, artists, design firms and major influencers in the arts.

"I had a cohort of mentors," she shares, noting that your mentor may not always look like you. "It's someone who believes in you, sees who you are and supports your potential." The guys next door to Tiana were a bit older; all of them were in equity research and eventually became venture capitalists. She asked them to teach her what she needed to know, what they were reading and what books they'd recommend.

Tiana tried several career choices in her quest to find her passion and the right career for her. Following her job with a design firm, Tiana worked for a leading international public relations firm and, later, an international auction house, where she found herself adrift in heavy seas in an industry and environment full of misogyny and racism. Tiana was a Director, working directly with the owners and the executive team, but it came with battle scars. "That experience was priceless. I learned so much about art and design history and the market," she acknowledges. "And I learned how to fight." With backstabbing and innuendo as everyday challenges, her life raft was in the relationships she made. "The value of allies is incredible," Tiana points out. Exhausted by the politics and the drama, she left, aware that she was more self-confident as a result of her auction world experience.

The success of Tiana's arts and cultural public relations firm is a testament to how she values relationships and what they have meant to her. At the same time that Tiana opened her doors, a friend that she had made at her first job also started a business and hired Tiana to represent her. This company has been with Tiana's firm for six years. "Be respectful, stay humble and connected to people," she advises.

"What excites you in your core?" she asks. "Follow what is in your heart! Don't live with regret. Take the time to find out where your passion lies. It may not necessarily be what you are good at. It might take you years to be good at it. The journey is soul-affirming and transformative."

Today Tiana is engaged in all aspects of her exciting life—both work and family—a life she envisioned when she opened her firm. "When your heart and your purpose are in alignment," Tiana observes, "this attracts the right opportunities and people." In Tiana's case, the alignment has helped her build strong relationships and a standout PR and branding firm.

Chapter 7
Learn How to Work

Observing, listening and learning from those
you respect will get you far.
No one expects you to know everything when you start.
Bring your common sense and a positive attitude and go to work.

Expect to be "onboarded"

Everyone knows how to work, don't they? Well...maybe. Imagine that you are hired for a job and when you show up to work on your first day there's no one there to tell you what to do or to help you in any way. How scared are you now?

Fortunately, the person who hired you is usually available to greet you and get you going or has asked an assistant to help show you the ropes. This is called "onboarding," bringing the new person along and making them feel comfortable in the organization.

Whether you are working online or in an office or physical environment, you'll be onboarded. Before you start work, it's good to know a few extra things about working.

Focus on what your boss expects from you

Of course, good work is the number one expectation. But there
are a few other things that your boss expects but may never say
out loud:

- **Confidentiality** – What's said at work stays at work
- **Loyalty** – You have their back at all times
- **Reliability** – You are dependable and trustworthy
- **Proactive thinking** – You're thinking ahead and
  preparing for the future, not just keeping up
- **Awareness** – You know what is happening in your area
  of the workplace and area of expertise
- **Curiosity** – You have an active mind that is looking for
  new and better answers, approaches, information and
  ideas

Ask questions and observe the culture

In getting her first jobs, Lynda Keeler claims she was "politely
persistent." Also, she had a little bravado. "I always presented
that I knew a little more than I did. Then I called on all of the
people I knew to learn all that I could."

You're new. You can't possibly know everything, and no one
expects you to. Ask lots of questions and if you are asking too
many, someone will tell you. The more you learn at the start, the
faster you will go. A good way to go is to jot your questions down
into a list so that you can get many answers in one quick session.

As you learn the ropes, continue to ask good questions—well-
chosen questions to well-chosen people. Find out all that you

can. Some companies have an organizational chart that they may share with you. If not, ask a bit from your "onboarder." It's okay to be curious as long as you are not intrusive. Knowing who does what and what the structure looks like will help you know where to go with your work and your questions.

While you're asking questions, be sure to learn how the phone and communications systems work! If you are working online or in a company large enough that you can't just yell down the hall, becoming adept with the phone and communications systems will score you big points and will keep you from having to depend on others to do simple tasks. The same is true of all conferencing systems and software. Master them and you become the master of your own communications.

Meanwhile, become a very good observer as you get started on your job. You'll learn a lot from just watching the work style and interactions of the people around you. They have a culture that is all theirs of which you are now a part.

Take notes and keep them

As you're asking questions, take notes of the answers. This ensures you won't have to ask the same question twice.

For projects, assignments and meetings, having a reference point as to what was asked of you will be hugely helpful. What are your responsibilities? Many are the times I have referred back to notes when there was a dispute about a detail like a printing quantity or delivery date and found the answer right there.

Bring your notebook, notepad or laptop with you to every meeting so that you are ready to take notes for later reference or follow-up. You're creating the context for the work you will be doing and for recording important information. As I am making notes, I like to make a star next to every "action item" so that I am sure to follow up. It makes life at work much easier. I keep my notes until a project is completed and delivered, and sometimes for reference long after.

Maintain a "to do" list

Mary Ackermann Gaer says this is an "always" way to work. Add new items that come in and cross off items as you accomplish them. Sort your list by "today," "this week" and "ongoing." Enjoy the satisfaction of updating the list each day before you leave work as you cross off the items you've accomplished and add new challenges for tomorrow.

Use reference materials

Reference materials are there to help you. For example, if you don't know how to set up a business letter, go online to find a format and bookmark it for future reference. Don't guess about business correspondence, as there are very real guidelines for letters, memos and written documents. Communicating properly in writing makes you a pro from the start. Also, your company may have its own standardized formats. Your "onboarder" will know.

Download or buy a grammar book. A stumbling block for many employees is the apostrophe and where it belongs.

Knowing the difference between "it's" and "its," for example, makes a big difference in your written communication.

I know of one young woman who found it helpful as she started her career as a Doctor of Physical Therapy to keep the reference book she used to study for her licensing exam handy. When a patient presented with a diagnosis she did not yet have experience treating, she had something to immediately refer to.

Like this young woman, don't hesitate to surround yourself with the reference tools you need and refer to them until you are comfortable without them.

Learn the difference between urgent and important

Some tasks are urgent and important, like making the airline reservation for a last-minute business trip when there are very few seats on the plane and your team is presenting to company shareholders. Some tasks are important but not urgent, like working on the new company logo design that everyone agrees needs to happen but doesn't have a deadline or timetable.

Urgent tasks have deadlines and require immediate attention. Important tasks advance the success of the business or long-term goals. To make an important task urgent, give it a deadline. Tasks that are urgent and important are things you must do right away or there will be serious consequences.

To be successful, learn how to segment your workload and work in these four categories:

- **Urgent and important** – Such as making your team's airline reservations for a presentation

- **Not urgent but important** – Your everyday action items at work that will advance the business and your career, such as working on the new logo
- **Urgent but not important** – Spending time putting out unimportant fires
- **Unimportant and not urgent** – Spending time doing things like checking personal email

While many things at work will be urgent, the ones that really matter are urgent and important. Learn the difference and keep your task lists accordingly. Aim to stay in the top two zones and use your productive hours for those tasks. Handle non-important tasks during slack times.

Create a tracking system or find one that works for you

Most everyone has their own way of working. Mine is to keep a master list of projects that is divided into tasks that are urgent and important, not urgent but important, urgent but not important, unimportant and not urgent. I segment my notepaper into four columns and make a list in each. I also keep a separate list of personal tasks. Writing things down gets them out of my mind and I get them done.

Every day I create a fresh list of what I'll tackle that day, often with times assigned for working on key projects so that I am sure to set aside enough time for them when I am fresh and at my best. Often, I do this before leaving work the day prior so that my mind is clear to enjoy my evening and I am fresh and "on point" when I sit down at work the next day.

You'll develop a system of your own. Many advanced systems are out there, handwritten and digital, pre-printed tracking systems and others created by management superstars. I've found that my simple system works best for me. You'll come up with something that works for you.

Get what you want out of each day

Organizing your activities the day prior helps. You can plan your work for tomorrow during the last half hour of today. Knowing what you are doing tomorrow enables you to structure the day to your maximum benefit and plan for any activities you'll undertake. Having a view of what's on the horizon, you can troubleshoot and then leave work behind to relax, knowing that you are ready for what's ahead tomorrow.

Plan ahead

If you're always behind or work "on deadline," set false deadlines and keep them. This is how people work on time. They allow enough time to complete the job before it is due, not "on deadline."

If you have a project due at 5:00 pm on Thursday, set a deadline for yourself of 5:00 pm on Tuesday. That will allow you to deliver on time no matter what happens. To be successful at this, you'll have to treat the Tuesday deadline as real, though, and not cheat yourself by slipping it back!

Be on time, which means be early

You are expected to be ready to start working on time, not to arrive then, so make a plan. Figure out how long it will take you to get there, get parked and in the door, get a cup of coffee and get going on time on your first day. And every day thereafter. It will be noticed!

Once I was waiting for a surf store to open at 8:30 am as advertised. It was for watersports gear. Those who surf and standup paddleboard know that often the most perfect water for their sports is early in the morning. Imagine their frustration when the clerk arrived at 8:30 am, unlocked the door, went in and locked it behind her while she "opened up," turning on the lights and cash register to prepare for work. Frustrated surfers waited in line outside for 15 minutes and when finally allowed in, were the grumpiest possible customers.

An advantage to being early is that you can troubleshoot anything that's going wrong and be the hero who emerges out of nowhere with the needed extension cord for the meeting or the markers that are missing for the board. While it may sound like you get to be the early-on-the-scene "gofer," you are actually the fixer and problem-solver, positioned as the person who's always "on it." Those people move faster in their careers.

Note, though, that if you are working as an hourly worker, unless you have prior authorization you most likely will not be paid for time worked "off the clock" that is before or after your official work hours. You cannot stretch or extend your paid work hours, but you can do extra unpaid work that will benefit your job and your employer depending on your circumstances. Before doing this, though, check with your employer to ensure you do not violate any rules, contracts or company policies.

In life you'll find that the early bird does get the worm in most everything. Arriving early at programs enables you to get the best seats and a chance to talk with the celebrity presenter. It enables you to hop on the best charter boat at the dock for the trip to the Great Barrier Reef. It helps you get the best seats with the most interesting people at dinner. Once you start arriving a bit early, you'll notice that you get noticed.

Be present

At work, cell phones and computers can take you right out of the present and into the personal. Be smart about your usage. You are at work to make a difference for the company and that's your focus. Save your personal phone calls and emailing for lunch and after work and you'll do a far better job. If your company has an employee handbook, refer to it regarding cell phone use at the office. This is real hot button with employers and it's important to find out from the start what is acceptable cell phone usage and what is not.

If you have children, bosses expect that you need to stay on top of communications. Come up with something that works for both of you and train your children not to interrupt you at work unless absolutely necessary. My mom was genius at this: She called us every day at our lunch hour for a short check-in. If we had important issues, we knew in advance we'd be talking at noon. Can you come up with a system that can work to keep everyone informed that's not interruptive?

Stop to analyze and think before tackling a large project

You have a huge task assigned to you. It's so large, you're shaking at the thought of how you can possibly get it done to begin with, and get it done on time, to boot! Let's assume that by now you've been working for a while. It's not your first assignment. Where do you start?

Steven Covey, author of "The 7 Habits of Highly Effective People," says it clearly: "Start with the end in mind." The first section of your plan will include a clear vision of the final product you are going to deliver, to whom it is to appeal and when and in what form it will be delivered. What does the final product look like and who and what are needed to get it there?

Get sign-off on this from your boss. When you have agreement up-front, you have a clear vision of the desired goals and can go to work making a written plan.

As the expression says, "How do you eat an elephant? One bite at a time." That's the same way you handle a large project. To plan for a large project, start with a responsibility checklist with due dates. This requires you to break a project down into steps, assign responsibilities and create deadlines. Again, when you start with the end in mind, you have an overview of the final product. Now you are slicing and dicing it in order to get it done and delivered.

Edit your work

Most of us write way too much. Simple words and short sentences say a lot with less. Blaise Pascal, a 17th century writer and scientist, said it well: "I have made this longer than usual because I have not had time to make it shorter."

In everything from emails to long reports, consider the first version to be your first draft. Take at least a few minutes away from it to come back and edit it down to a second draft. For big documents, create a third draft.

Leave white space by writing short paragraphs. This will keep your readers from hitting a huge, overwhelming wall of black type. Include subheads, as I did in this book. Subheads are like "visual signposts" that help guide the reader through the piece. White space and subheads also work in tandem to make your written piece look more inviting...which is a good thing.

Spell check every document you create. Before you print or send *any* document, make sure to spell check. The program is built into the software you are using...so use it!

Be proactive

Taking action before it's needed is what your boss is hoping for from you. It is having the self-confidence to address an issue in your area of work before it becomes a problem.

Bosses like to know what's happening around them. One of my favorite employees always brought me both the problem and the recommended solution with documentation or research to back things up. When asked at a meeting what it would cost if we moved our gala event from here to there, she simply pulled out her spreadsheet and gave the answer. She was on it...in advance.

Dress for the occasion

If you know that VIPs are attending the online meeting or coming through the office on Tuesday, plan your wardrobe in advance to look your very best that day. You never know who is watching. It could be someone with influence who is watching your appearance and behavior and how you might fit in a higher role.

When you have outside appointments, a good rule of thumb is to dress one notch higher than the normal dress for that organization. You can get a feel for how people dress there by checking out their website for work photos, looking on LinkedIn for the company profile or asking your boss or a co-worker about what the culture is like.

Cool off after tough incidents

In a career there are many times it seems right to quit out of frustration or anger rather than cooling off to really analyze and solve the problem that created those emotions within you. Once you finish with a tough situation, take a break or a walk away from the incident. Just get out of there. Don't talk to others on your way out the door. If you can, get outside and cool off. One time I actually went clothes shopping for two hours. Then I returned and did my job.

Don't write a memo about it. Don't try to solve this with email. If you feel compelled to put it all in writing to absolve yourself or tell your side of the story, then write it but DO NOT SEND IT. Save it. Let it sit overnight, then delete it the next day. You don't need and you do not ever want to engage in an

YES! YOU CAN DO IT!

email war or write something emotional that will later be used against you.

Try to check your emotions

Can you cry at work? I don't believe there's a rule on this one. I have. Once I was incredibly frustrated because I was promised a raise and the money was not in my check. I felt betrayed and forgotten. Stupid me, it was just the bookkeeper's mistake. Once you get to an executive level, you are paid to set an example and be in control of your emotions. Sometimes, though, things happen.

Colby Fisher Dailey says she does cry. "I get emotional," she says, "because I care." And that can be because of disappointment or joy.

Value everyone in the workplace

Everyone with whom you work has value and they will know immediately how you value them. For example, nothing is more important to all of us than to be known by our names. So learn names right from the start. Calling others by their name communicates respect and helps them know that they are recognized as individuals. It is the first step to developing friendships and relationships. When you treat everyone from the front desk employee to the CEO with equal respect, you will watch your career path turn into an escalator.

"Sometimes the people you work with will end up being the people you work for," says Lynda Keeler who went from working with a small CNN team in San Diego to CNN's large team in San Francisco. Her good relationships propelled her forward.

Respond quickly

Value your relationships by responding quickly to calls and inquiries. For requests from your boss, likely you will need to respond immediately. For others, respond the same day for most inquiries or within 24 hours. If you need more information to respond to an inquiry, let the person know that you have their request and are getting an answer back to them as soon as possible. Say what you can do, not what you can't, and then do it.

Learn how to say, "I don't know but I'll find out." These words are your friends. You're just starting, and no one expects you to know everything. "I don't know but I'll find out," is a great answer. It tells the person that you are working with that you are truthful and there to do the job. Once you do find out, follow up immediately.

See that you are part of a team

If you've played team sports you already understand that the team wins the game or match, not the individual. In most work situations, you are working as part of a team. Respect your team leader. Should you disagree with their position, share your thoughts privately with them. Don't do it in a non-team meeting or presentation. A basic rule is team players stick together in public.

How many times have you been in a meeting when someone from your team makes a point and comments on something you've all agreed upon, and then a rogue member has to "add on?" No matter how hard, resist the temptation. Let others' final comments stand.

Sometimes you'll have to take one for the team. You can air your thoughts outside and in private, but in a meeting with a team presentation, your job is to stick with the team and agree. When you are on a team, the team position is more valuable than yours. Follow the leader and do the job you set out to do together.

Give others the information they need to do their job

Let's say that you are responsible for getting some vendors paid but haven't yet worked with the financial person or controller on your team. If you have a purchase order (P.O.) system, you'll be asked to fill one out for each check to be issued. You'll provide the full information regarding the vendor and the product or service delivered. Once you properly fill out and submit the P.O., the right wheels start turning and a check is issued.

When you deal with your workload in this fashion, by providing the full information required by your co-workers so that they can follow up and do their part, whether it's a financial transaction or something entirely different, it gets done in one simple effort. You'll move much faster through your work and co-workers will appreciate working with you because they can do their job.

Understand and respect the office hierarchy

It may take some time to learn the channels, but it's worth it. The people around you will be resentful if you jump over them— and believe me, you will hear about it.

Organizations have defined pathways to make work most efficient and to make sure that work is going to the proper people. While sometimes you will want to jump protocol and get an answer to a simple question by "going direct" to the person with the answer, you may need to follow a prescribed path.

For example, if you are in marketing and need an answer from an executive in budgeting, you may need to go through that person's assistant to either set a time to talk together or to provide the question so that it can be answered. In this case, do not "jump over" the assistant and just go directly to the budget executive. If you do, you will surely upset someone in the food chain.

Be prepared for the Hell Curve

You've heard of the bell curve. In the first year of work, you'll be riding on the Hell Curve. It's the simple progression of four 13-week periods of learning. Here's how it works:

- *Week 1 through 13*
  This is your honeymoon period. It's when you meet everyone, learn who is who in the pecking order and where things are. Most everyone is kind and smiley and friendly because you're the "newbie." It's a fun period. "Gee, this is good," you're likely to think.

- *Week 13–25*

  This is an intensifying period. You're going uphill. You've been on the job for long enough now that your boss and teammates are expecting work out of you, good work. You still don't know a lot of things, but they give you allowance for that.

- *Week 26–39*

  You've reached the top of the roller coaster and are now headed into the downward curve. At this point, your boss and team have been working with you for over six months. By now, they are expecting you to know a lot about what you are doing, what the business is doing, who to go to with problems and/or solutions. The expectations are far higher now. It can be a bit scary and you may have feelings of "What am I doing here? They need someone who can help them." Hang in there.

- *Week 40 through 52*

  Still on a downward curve, you are expected to really know things you don't know but now you have the wherewithal to find out and respond back. It's a bit rougher and can be a tough time, but you are handling it.

- *Week 53*

  You've made it! Week 53 is the start of your second year...

Congratulations! By the completion of Year One you have truly learned how to work. It's all uphill from here. The people around you are pleased with their investment in teaching you because you are taking off. Headed into Year Two, you are starting to have fun, perhaps even training the "newbies" just like your team trained you. You are fully on your way. It's a great time to work because you know the routines, you anticipate what's coming and are prepared. Now you can take on new challenges!

Enjoy more after your first year

By the end of your first year you have the other things in place, too.

After a year of building a work wardrobe and perhaps buying some colorful shoes your closet is full, and you can spend your resources on other things that may be more fun. Your circle of friends has grown, and you know lots of interesting people. They may be part of your life for a very long time. You have new skills and the confidence to use them.

Enjoy Year Two. It's your year of achievement. If you stay in this job, relax a little but work a lot. During this year, you can experience your job and your life without the stress of starting over again somewhere else. It may be the start of many years with this employer. You have earned vacation time and have the funds to travel. Also, your employer has invested in you, and it's nice to pay that back with hard work. It's not yet time to move on. Investing at least two years in a job is a good move and an indicator to future employers that you are not a "job hopper."

Give it your all

When you give it your all day after day, work often pays you back. That's what happened to Lynda Keeler.

Lynda built a name in cable TV and the internet as an early pioneer by being in the right place at the right time and learning all that she could before everyone else. She started her career at a jewelry store but her "learn it all" attitude and passion for her work took her into the stratosphere of emerging technology.

"Right out of college, I went into the management training program of Shreve & Company," she says. "It was like a finishing school located in downtown San Francisco and I loved it." Shreve touts itself as "San Francisco and Palo Alto's trusted jeweler since 1852." Lynda lived nearby and took a cable car to work. Then, after nine months of training, she was assigned to serve as Assistant Manager in a suburban mall store one hour from downtown. "It was night and day...a challenge physically to get there, limited interactions with interesting people and not exciting at all."

At the same time, she was immersed in friendships with people who talked about computers and technology. "They knew coding. What they didn't know was marketing." A friend alerted her to a job opening in the nascent cable industry. "Entertainment and technology...what a mix!" she exclaims. Lynda joined a small cable company at the birth of a brand-new industry, using her marketing skills to introduce CNN and HBO to viewers unaccustomed to paying for TV.

Offered a bigger opportunity, she moved to San Diego. "In every job, I work to learn the technology, the nuts and bolts of what goes on in each department," she says. "Whether it is repair or programming, I want a holistic understanding of the business." Passionate about her new career, she worked every weekend and volunteered at company events.

"To be part of a new initiative is an exciting thing to do... getting in the door before it's an established industry. Things move fast, you learn a lot. The rules are still being made. Working with an energized, emerging industry...it's exhilarating!"

Lynda Keeler

Lynda headed into brand-new industries where she could make the rules.

"Work for companies you are really proud of," says digital media pioneer Lynda Keeler. That advice has propelled her hugely successful career.

Lynda credits much of her success to building and maintaining good relationships at all levels—with her superiors, co-workers, vendors and everyone who touched her work life.

Lynda carefully made her moves up the ladder from her start in the management training program of Shreve & Company jewelers in San Francisco to a small cable TV provider in San Diego, working with the team from CNN. When she had an offer from CNN in the Bay area, she took it. "When you move, there are a lot of ripple effects," she observes. "In leaving, I did not go to work for a competitor, so my move up looked good for my boss, who was my mentor. He has remained a friend."

Later, Lynda returned to Southern California to work for HBO, a perfect fit, where she stayed for 10 years. "If you can get at least one big brand name on your resume," Lynda asserts, "others feel that you are vetted. They'll think, 'If she worked for them, then she's been proven.'" In Lynda's case, CNN and HBO "gave her two extra cards in her deck."

Moving forward at HBO, Lynda was promoted into a job where she was in charge of affiliate relations for HBO, managing client relationships in what was then the "man's world" of cable TV. That meant traveling and entertaining, i.e. taking clients to lunch or dinner on the HBO expense account. She had simple rules that worked for her. "I never drank with dinner or let the conversation get too close to personal issues," Lynda explains. "I never dressed provocatively, and, though I was a single woman, I always had an extra ring I could slip on if needed. I wanted to keep a bit of distance." Lynda adds that letting those you work with know too much about you gives them knowledge that can potentially be used against you.

Lynda's favorite job was as Executive Vice President at Sony Pictures. "From 1994 to 2000, they were inventing the internet," she says. "It was the early days, the Wild West. Everything was new, there were no rules, and I was at a big movie studio where we had lots of freedom. We were making it up and it was fantastic!" Lynda started with a division of 20 people that she soon grew to 200.

Always fascinated with business, Lynda learned how to work by being observant, studying people and watching their interactions. And she learned what she loved and what she didn't. For example, she once took a job as a venture capitalist. "I knew nothing about the VC world," she admits, "and lasted one year before returning to Sony to work at the corporate level." Asked about going back, she said, "When you burn a bridge you have to figure out how much of the wood you want to burn because sometimes you may want to go back across."

I first met Lynda through a friend and can see that she values her friendships now as much as she has valued relationships throughout her career.

Chapter 8
Work Closely With Your Boss to Achieve Success

Your strong working relationships can advance
your career for a lifetime.

Work harder than ever

Getting your job was the easy part. Now that you have it, you'll want to work harder than ever. "The harder you work, the luckier you get," says Jennifer Slaughter. "Hard work earns trust in you from leaders and that opens doors and gives you the freedom to set your own agenda. That's gold."

Focus on building a good working relationship with your boss

This relationship can be a long-term asset. Why? Because the people with whom you forge good working relationships—your work mentors, peers and contacts—stay with you and follow you throughout your career. Your boss and your "tribe" may serve as references for you in getting a new job either in the immediate future or a long way down the road. If you are fortunate to have a good boss who is a strong mentor, this person may introduce you to their network, where you will meet even more people that offer a myriad of opportunities for your later career.

Building a strong working relationship with your boss will help you get the job done and will make it more fun and challenging. When you know where you are headed, you can get there.

Expect these things from your boss as you build your work relationship

- **Guidance** – Providing the information you need to do the job you are asked to do
- **Feedback** – Meeting with you on a continuing basis to help you improve your work, sharing the positive and the negative
- **Respect** – Good treatment, always
- **Loyalty** – Having your back just as you have theirs
- **Opportunity** – Providing challenges to help you learn, grow and advance

Communicate regularly with your boss

Excellent people in fabulous jobs can often lose it all because they don't communicate, while seemingly modest people move into superstar roles because they are good at communication. Good communication is a primary component of success in your career.

You might be worried about communicating too much, but don't be. Set on a path to keep your boss informed and see what happens. If you are overcommunicating, your boss will let you know. And you can always ask, "Am I communicating too frequently or providing too much information?" Meet and exceed expectations and communicate as you do so.

Set up regular meetings and check-ins with your boss

Many bosses who appear to be too busy to meet with you on an unscheduled basis will readily agree to a short daily or weekly meeting. Scheduled meetings offer a way to build a productive, collaborative relationship. Also, they facilitate managing a large workload by providing you with access to the boss on a regular basis.

At the start of a new job, if you can get 15 minutes daily from your boss at the same time each day, you'll be doing great. And, if you can schedule a longer meeting of 30 to 60 minutes at the same time every Monday to review the work of the coming week, you'll really be ahead of the game. Scheduled meetings with your boss enable you to ask questions, understand what success looks like to your boss and achieve results together. That builds a strong work connection.

It's possible that your boss conducts a regular weekly team check-in meeting. If you are not on the list of invitees, it's okay to ask if you might be added, especially if you are responsible for following up on events and activities for your boss that result from the team meeting. If you are not included, don't worry. You will soon discover in which meetings you belong. It won't be every meeting!

If regular meetings are not possible, keep a list of things you'd like to discuss. When you are invited in the door or on the phone, deal with the most important and urgent items first. Then, you may be able to move on to the less important items. If there is not time, you have gotten done what you needed to do.

Create no surprises for your boss

Bosses like to confidently go forward every day with trust in their team. Surprises, even little things, can throw off their day and their confidence in you, especially if the boss is thrown into a situation for which they are unprepared. Let's say your boss always runs an introductory client meeting with place cards on the conference table printed on both sides so it is easy to call everyone by name. One day, you provide stick-on badges instead, believing they will improve socialization during the coffee hour prior. During the meeting, your boss is unable to read the name badges and it alters their very personal style. Later, they are upset with you. However, if you tell your boss your idea in advance, your boss may agree and ask you to provide both...the name badges and the name cards.

Bosses don't need or want surprises. They are bosses because they make smart choices. Run things past your boss, even if you believe that your ideas are better than what's been done in the past. Maybe they are, and you'll get credit for your thinking. Or perhaps what you suggest has been tried and didn't work. Either way, you'll learn, and your boss will appreciate that you are problem-solving.

Do it in one glop, not spoonfuls

We had a manager for one of our business operations who used to ping us constantly for many things that could have been dealt with in a group. Working with her wasted everyone's time and consisted of constant daily interruptions—until she got smart and made lists that could each be dealt with in one five-minute meeting or email. Keeping lists will help you do many things at once, especially when you require oversight or approvals to get your job done. Value your co-workers' time and they will value you.

Listen to what your boss wants

Sometimes you may be asked to do something or find out something that you believe is minor in importance but, for some reason, is major to your boss. However, your boss did not tell you that. You will find out the second time your boss asks. Just change-up your attitude about whatever the matter is and take care of it. If you don't, despite all of the wonderful things you do and accomplish, by the third time you are asked you will know that it's one thing upon which your boss is focused. Handle it and handle it fast because until it's done, it may be the only thing your boss can see.

Keep it positive

You can frame things to keep them positive even amidst the worst storm. It sets you off as professional, not emotional, when you refrain from making or writing negative comments, especially about co-workers.

If you are ever tempted to put something negative into a memo or correspondence or to point a finger at someone, back away from the computer before you push "send." Walk around the block. And then come back and erase it. There is always a way to reframe things or simply use facts but not accusations.

"Be aware of how you phrase things," says Lynda Keeler. "Think through your communication and what your memos and emails really say to the person who receives them."

Bosses like problem-solvers, so the trick is to move away from finger pointing into solving problems. The technique is to state what went or is going wrong and provide a realistic proposed solution to fix it. "The gizmo order came in later than scheduled, but we can deliver on schedule if we tighten up our production schedule by one day," will get you much further than stating "Joe forgot to order the gizmos and put the whole project off schedule and now it's a mess."

When you are asked about problems, be honest, but do your best to be a team player and minimize finger pointing by providing good solutions instead. Employees who bring a proposed solution to the boss along with the problem go far!

Keep excuses to yourself

For example, if you mess up and are late, you may want to keep your excuses to yourself. Providing too much information ("TMI") can trip you up. One of the best things about being an adult is that you no longer need to explain "why." Just say, "I'm sorry that I am late," and get to work. And then make whatever changes you need to make in your life to keep you from being late again.

If you have a project that won't be completed on time, let your boss know in advance. Forget any excuses and get the work done. According to self-help guru Jim Rohn, "If you really want to do something, you'll find a way. If you don't, you'll find an excuse."

Find a good mentor and keep learning

Tiana Webb Evans says it simply: "Many young graduates are disconnected from the idea of a journey. They expect success to happen immediately, not understanding that it's a process. So many 25-year-olds expect to be able to do my job in the first week! I am always amused." Tiana spends approximately 30% of each workday mentoring and coaching her team.

When you interview for a job you're looking for many things, and one of them is a good mentor, someone who will teach you. While it may be tempting to tackle something where you have a lot of responsibility right at the start, if you are in a new field, you'll want someone to learn from. Look at the job in a holistic way. What is the job? Where can you go for help? Are you working with someone that will be there to help you get started, help you along the way and assist in bailing you out when you mess up, as you are practically guaranteed to do?

Recognize that relationships can go sour

When things go sour with a co-worker who may be jealous or trying to sabotage you in some way, understand that the person is a bit weak. It doesn't make dealing with them any easier, but if you know that you can take a "higher road" and would never stoop to their level, it gives you the tools to work with them or work without them.

If you need to engage your boss, ask for advice. Don't complain. Ask for advice as in, "This is happening. How do you suggest I deal with it?" Bosses like to be asked for advice because they are there to make things work and want to untangle problems or issues that are getting in the way of work. But it's best if you do the tough work, the untangling, instead of passing it off to your boss.

Why? Because involving your boss may take things to a whole new level.

If you have a good boss, that boss will give you useful advice and keep checking on your progress. If the problems persist, you can ask the boss to become involved. This is a bit of dangerous ground because it will bring things to the forefront in a conversation that you may not like. Remember, each party has a side that they believe to be valid. So, think hard before asking your boss to become involved in a "personality" situation because you may not like what happens.

Bosses, especially at large companies, keep personnel records and files and may write memos that go into your file for reference. Your file will follow you throughout your career there. Sometimes, it's best not to have problematic situations in your file. It all depends on the circumstances.

A special circumstance is anything involving sexual or other harassment, which is illegal. Don't keep it to yourself, take it to your boss. If your boss is the harasser, go to your boss' boss. Do not delay in this.

Disagree with your boss if you understand how to do it

Bosses are usually right because they have a lot of experience to bring to a situation. Sometimes, however, your work can be subjective and there is no right answer, just many good answers. If you are passionate about a project and disagree with your boss, you may want to talk with them about your thoughts on a specific topic or situation.

To disagree and make your opinion known, do the following:

- **Acknowledge** that you both share the same goal, to create an outstanding result, and that there really is no right answer here.
- **Calmly outline** your reasons for supporting another course of action or solution, making it clear that you will defer to whatever your boss wants.
- **Follow up** as you have agreed together.

Both of you have the best interests of the company in mind, and by discussing alternate solutions, you may learn a lot about both your boss and your company.

Deal with a bad boss

Bad bosses happen. Sometimes you are hired by one and then that boss who hired you leaves only to be replaced by a bad boss. Or perhaps you are promoted into an exciting new job and your new boss and you are like oil and water. The best thing you can do is wait it out for a while and let things settle down. Don't start complaining to your co-workers, because things get around quickly at work. Give your new boss a chance and give yourself a chance. Try to make it through three solid months to see how it goes as you try to figure out what's happening and why.

Picky bosses want things done in a certain way and it's wise to adjust to that way even though you believe your way is better. It's possible that influences are happening behind the scene that are not evident to you at this time.

After giving it a good try, you may conclude that you just have a ragged relationship and it's time to sit down and talk about what's happening. For this discussion and other sensitive ones, change the venue if possible, to get your boss out from behind their desk so you are more equal. Schedule an off-site cup of coffee together, for example, or meet in a conference room. Move your boss away from their power position in the hopes of achieving a more open environment and discussion.

I've had several great bosses, a few good ones and a couple of bad ones. Through it all, I have believed that life is too short to stay with the bad ones if things cannot be fixed and there is no room to move elsewhere in the organization. Go find a better one. In Chapter 12 we'll talk about how to evaluate your situation and move forward.

Chapter 9
Know That You Belong

Know that you have worked hard to get where you are.
Remain strong. Believe in yourself and you will open doors
in your life and career.

Expect some early successes and failures

One of the best ways to deal with your career is to be the best version of yourself every day.

Just as you will have early successes, you'll also have early failures. "In life things come together and they fall apart," says Jennifer Slaughter. "Enjoy the highs and know that the lows will pass."

Tiana Webb Evans views work as a journey. "The magic does not happen immediately," she says, "but it will happen if you are committed to the process."

Share your successes

Most of your workplace successes will in some ways connect directly back to your team. It's a rare project that is completed by one person and one person alone. Of course, it happens, but it might not happen without the path having been cleared or the unselfish support of others.

When you have success and the opportunity to take praise for a project, remember those who helped you and include them in your comments and thanks. You've seen it on the Academy Awards. Your response will be a mini response but hit the same chords. What you want to communicate is: "I did not do this alone. I did it with my team." Be proud of your accomplishments but be humble as well. It's the best teambuilding you can do.

Also, don't be afraid to be there for your co-workers as you hope they will be there for you.

When you share your authentic self with others and enjoy their successes with them and are also there to support them through their failures, you give them the gift of getting to know you in your best light.

Learn from your failures

"Experience is what you got when you didn't get what you wanted," says one of my favorite T-shirts. Failure is how you learn. Or, as Tiana Webb Evans puts it, "Failure is information, not the end of your life."

So many of us are unnecessarily hard on ourselves for making simple mistakes and failing at unimportant things. Don't be that person. If you make a mistake, correct it and apologize, if needed, but don't dwell on it. Shake it off. This is life and it is a long and winding path.

Quite a bit of new research is out about the benefits of early failures in helping to build careers. No one achieves success at everything, and likely you won't either. Failure often means that you got outside of your comfort zone and tried new things. That, in itself, is success.

If you have hurt someone or their relationships or career by something you have done, whether your actions were intentional or unintentional, don't let things sit. Get in front of your co-worker right away and humbly apologize. Email and phone calls are poor substitutes for meeting with people in person to apologize when you can. If you can't meet, calling is the next best option. Emailing an apology works, but only email as a last resort.

We are all human and we make mistakes. Treat others as you would like to be treated. Nothing trumps the most personal, face-to-face approach in these situations. Saying "I'm sorry" while looking someone in the eye is the best and biggest thing you can do.

Know that you're not an imposter

Imagine that you are invited to attend a meeting with the head of your company and your mind flashes, "Should I really be here?" The buttons on the boss' black blazer are reflected in your panicked eyes and your brain is off the grid. You are doubting everything you have done to get here and are convinced that your boss is going to find out you are a fraud. Breathe deeply. Just breathe. Have you ever heard of Imposter Syndrome? You're not having a panic attack. You're just doubting yourself. So, pull it together. Yes. You can do it!

The fact is that you belong. All of your preparation and hard work got you there. You are not an imposter. What you must do is breathe deeply, calm down and when you get out of the meeting, give yourself a few moments to get yourself together. Then you must start to reflect on how you got there and what good work you are doing. Make a list of your accomplishments so far. If you have a trusted friend or a fan, confide in them to receive some positive feedback. You are not alone in this and you will be okay.

In my favorite photo of my mom, the fashion designer/ championship tennis player Harriet Fisher, she's posed front and center at the net surrounded by the University of Toledo men's tennis team. Yes, the men's team. The University of Toledo had no women's team, so she tried out and played with the men. In that era, 1939, another university refused to play them so as not to risk defeat by a woman, so she gracefully resigned. She wasn't a feminist; she just loved to play tennis and saw no reason she could not play for her university. Poised and charming, my mother simply believed that she belonged, quietly tried out and earned her position. From her, I learned that you can belong wherever you want until someone or something knocks you out, and even then, you have choices in how to deal with it.

Reframe your negative thoughts

Perhaps you're scared or intimidated or believe that perhaps you are not worthy of the job you've earned and are in. It's perfect for you, but you've hit a speedbump that makes you doubt yourself.

Ocean rower and adventurer Roz Savage wasn't working at a job when she learned how to reframe her thinking, though it's a skill you may want to use. Asked about her greatest accomplishment, she'll readily respond, "Rowing the Atlantic. It was SO hard." Then she adds that, of course, she had chosen to be there. Hard days led to insights that, in turn, made them into good days. One insight was that she could reframe things. It was when she had tendonitis, saltwater sores, broken equipment and had just eaten the last of her snack bars that she remembered that she had wanted to get out of her comfort zone. So the fact that she was feeling miserable wasn't a sign of failure, it was a sign of success. In short, yes, she was miserable. "But," as she says, "getting outside of your comfort zone is, by definition, going to be uncomfortable."

According to Roz, "Being uncomfortable makes us better, stronger people." While she was "miserable as hell," she told herself that she would be grateful for this experience. Her bravery is a good example of how to feel "wobbly" about something but go for it anyway.

Reframing your thoughts is an important skill when you finally get that job you've sought. You may be working and not rowing the Atlantic, you may have doubts, but you're there, you're in the mix and you are ready to go on and build a successful career.

ROZ SAVAGE

Roz has an ocean of tenacity and wisdom.

Standing on the stage at Telluride Mountainfilm, the small blond woman behind the podium put up a slide of herself in small rowboat amidst a raging sea. It was Rosalind ("Roz") Savage, ocean rower, writer and speaker, holder of four

Guinness records for ocean rowing and the first woman to row solo across the "Big Three" oceans—the Atlantic, Pacific and Indian. Named a National Geographic Adventurer of the Year following her Pacific crossing in 2010, Roz looked very happy on that stage as she shared a film and the story of her adventures.

Roz is a force in nature, appointed a Member of the Order of the British Empire for her services to fundraising and the environment. She has a twinkle in her eye and a strong sense of humor that she brings to her observations on meaning and mystery in life, developed during over 500 days alone at sea in a 23-foot rowboat.

Roz started her career on a far different, more predictable path, on land. After receiving her law degree from Oxford, she worked as a management consultant. "It was so constraining," she recalls. "I had grown up in a family without much money and I had believed that money might buy me happiness. But I was absolutely miserable."

She says that "What Color is Your Parachute," the popular book on careers, didn't work for her at all. Not much did until she was introduced to self-improvement author Stephen Covey and his book, "The 7 Habits of Highly Effective People." His tenet, "start with the end in mind" hit home with Roz. "It's about where you want to end up," she realized, "not where do you go from here." An exercise in writing her own obituary reminded Roz that she was merely mortal and gave her the kick she needed to change.

Roz wrote two versions of her obituary during one hour of an otherwise ordinary evening. One version reflected the life she wanted and one reflected where she was heading for if she carried on the life she was currently leading. When she wrote the first version, the life she wanted, Roz was thinking freely about a life that was radically different, and about becoming a person dramatically different than the one she was at the time. She went from someone with nose-diving self-esteem to becoming someone who was go-getting and "indomitable."

"It felt really real," she shares. "It opened a door to a parallel universe. I was living the life I was supposed to be living. I had given my soul an opportunity to express its deepest longing. I suspended reality. What was the life that I yearned to live? It flowed out." Then reality and self-limiting talk came in and Roz put her written obituary away in a drawer for two years. "The brain likes to keep us safe," she comments. "It likes to keep us small. The soul sees the bigger picture."

Roz's change was gradual. She quit her job, left her marriage and traveled abroad in what she calls her "happy dabbling period." She journeyed solo to Peru where she wrote a book. "I was outside of my comfort zone," she admits. "I didn't speak Spanish and had never backpacked before."

Prior to setting out in that rowboat on the Atlantic, Roz undertook an exercise adapted from the military: She ran through every possible scenario of what could go wrong and developed plans to address them. What if there was a hole in the boat? What if the camping stove set things on fire? What if she capsized and could not get back up? "I thought of it all in advance," she says, "which gave me the confidence to see it all through. This was important!"

Of all her successes, crossing the Atlantic is the biggest to Roz. It was her first ocean, and it was the hardest. "A massive learning curve," is what she calls it. She'd dedicated her life savings and was "all in." Naive optimism and stubborn pride got her through, and "faith, not fear."

I am grateful to Roz for her speaking and writing, including her TED talks; her work for the environment, sustainability and women; and her blog posts and books.

Roz' advice to young women starting careers is simple. "Stop taking yourself so seriously. Live your life as if knowing that nothing matters at all. Most decisions are fixable," says the woman who set off in a boat on three oceans on her own. If anyone should know, it's Roz.

Find Roz' obituary exercise in Appendix 7 or download it at www.NancyWilhelms.com.

Move past old, preconceived notions about yourself

One of the most dynamic women I have known went from hair stylist to multi-millionaire. Jan Anderson claims that she got her "Ph.D. in women" during 14 years as a hair stylist, and then her "Ph.D. in men and math" during 17 years as a financial planner. In direct selling (think products like Nu Skin, Body Wise and Mary Kay) she blended those two professions together, and Jan and her husband Jerry became a powerhouse duo.

When asked what she believes contributes to finding an abundant life path, Jan's answer is, "Be a clean slate. If you let your past define you, it can hold you back and make you un-coachable and slower to adapt and accelerate."

Jan saw herself living the life and lifestyle of a millionaire long before she left small town Corsicana, Texas and made it materialize in San Diego. She made it a point to tap into the feeling level of her body. Every day as she and her husband headed to work she pretended that they were making $77,000 per month and solving all of their problems from that point of feeling successful. She visualized herself walking across a stage in front of hundreds of people to accept an award. It worked.

Asked about common traits amongst those who don't succeed, she says that the tendency to define yourself by your past, your family and friends and your current circumstances can be a negative. She tapped into the power of her dreams and consistently worked toward them every day, knowing that she could have them.

And she does!

Believe in yourself and in what you can do

A lot of "getting things done" can happen by just looking and talking like you know what you are doing because...you do. Have you ever watched others head for the front of a long line to be admitted to a party or restaurant simply because they looked right and acted assured? Sometimes, just playing the role will take you where you want to go. How many starlets were plucked from obscurity by having that "certain something"? In business, it's called "executive presence." When you see it, you know it. Study those around you that have it and learn by listening and watching. The methodology is simple: Believe in yourself and act accordingly.

Watch for opportunities where you work...and prepare to get them

Your next job could be one office away. Just keep your eyes and ears open for opportunity where you work. When it arrives, it pays to be ready to interview with a current resume and the right approach.

If you have the opportunity to interview for another job within your company, even if you work in a casual firm and know your interviewer, remember that it is still a job interview. You are not showing up just to talk. Arrive as you would for a formal interview, with the same preparation, including a portfolio and samples and examples of your work. Treat the interview as if you had never interviewed there before, and don't assume that since they know you, you'll get the job.

Network whenever you can; belong beyond your company

Through networking, you can belong to something larger—not just your company, but your industry, where you can meet your peers and broaden your world perspective as part of a much larger universe...where you belong. Learn about professional and trade organizations associated with your industry and ask management if they will sponsor you for a local membership. Joining industry groups enables you to learn about the newest trends and issues, and meet the movers and shakers while making new friends. Growing your own peer group will help you succeed at whatever you endeavor.

Chapter 10
Trust Your Instincts and Stay With Your Values

You'll encounter some challenging situations. Trust yourself...you'll know what to do.

Make values-based decisions and
you'll end up in the right places

Project Manager Mary Ackermann Gaer was on a construction jobsite when a cement mixer arrived with a bad load. Each batch of concrete is tested before pouring to be certain that the mix is correct. "If it contains too much water, it won't have the strength required to support the floor above it," she explained. This batch failed the "slump test" so Mary told them to stop and send the truck back. The supervisor was not on the site and Mary had to make a decision. "I got a lot of 'pushback' from the contractor to ignore things and let the load be poured," she said. "I went back to the office, made two calls and shut the job down."

Later, working for a national homebuilder in customer service, Mary kept track of all of the complaint calls. "They didn't like that at all," she recalls. As a licensed general contractor, Mary pointed out quality issues, yet her advice and recommendations were ignored. "They wanted a 'yes man' to keep customers out of their hair." Mary lasted six months with the "good old boys" and then went on to start her own home inspection business to do the work she was not able to do there.

As she says, "If things don't feel right, they aren't, so keep moving forward."

You know what feels right and what feels wrong. It's an awareness that will serve you well. Minor challenges can actually be defining moments in careers.

MARY ACKERMANN GAER

Mary pursued her passion into a man's world that did not want women.

Always interested in how things are built, Mary Ackerman Gaer started her career as a cost accounting clerk for a Southern California developer that built chain restaurants for major brands. Mary soon learned how to do accounts payable, payroll and whatever they needed. "My work ethic was passed on by my father, a German engineer," she observes. "You do whatever you need to do even if it's not in your job description. Go beyond and your life will be more interesting." As she grew her experience and talents, Mary believed that she'd be promoted. But she wasn't. They were afraid to have people work for a woman.

Mary went on to become a safety manager, working on the jobsite of a sewage treatment plant in the trailers and on the dirt. And she began learning everything she could about construction. When Mary and her husband added a room addition to their house, she learned first-hand about paint, insulation and all of the components that go into a residence.

Seeking to grow and change her life, Mary enrolled in an intensive self-help program. Her takeaway was self-talk that had a simple message: Whatever you are doing, it's your choice and the consequences of that choice are also yours. Mary has lived by that lesson ever since.

Now working with greater self-confidence, Mary became the first female project manager at a new firm, where she was put in charge of construction of a large office park. Regardless of her job description, Mary made only half of what her male counterparts earned because, she was told, she didn't have a college degree. Changing her prospects with a bold move to Sacramento, Mary landed a job on a public housing project building 1,500 low-income housing units. "I got a good job because of affirmative action," she relates, "finally getting around the wage inequality barriers I experienced."

Working in management in her field required either a degree or a general contractor's license, so Mary took classes and applied her years of on-the-job experience to meet the qualifications to earn the license. "It was as intense as it could be," Mary shares. "When I walked into a huge conference center to take the test, 2,000 men turned around to look at me and the four other women." With her license in hand, Mary doubled her salary overnight.

Mary's experience in building public housing made her a strong believer in the opportunities offered by working in the government. "When you get into a government job, you

YES! YOU CAN DO IT!

can work your way up," she says. "Environmental projects, the Coast Guard...there are good places to go. And once you earn a good salary in a job, it's far easier to go higher and earn more. Letters of recommendation always help."

Mary went on to open her own home inspection business and today is among the most successful Realtors in Southern California. That's where I met her. My husband and I have bought three houses working together with Mary.

Along the way, Mary did finally earn her college degree. "It was on my bucket list," she admits. "My dad always wanted us to have college degrees." Today she holds not one but two college degrees: one in business management and one in marketing.

Accept only good behavior

Your bosses are persons of influence and their space on the work totem pole is higher than yours. Your boss can be fired and sued for improper use of their influence. Many workplaces have written sexual harassment policies and guidelines to address these very issues, and the federal laws are very clear. Sexual discrimination and harassment are against the law.

If you are working for a company with more than a handful of employees, it may have an employee handbook that deals with what's okay in working there and what is not. Use it as your first point of reference. It will tell you how to proceed if you have a complaint or are being sexually harassed.

Don't believe that you have to say that you're sorry to some associate who is trying to touch or get close to you. This goes for male and female bosses and co-workers. Predators of both sexes, equally charming, are out there.

If you are the victim of sexual harassment, do not delay documenting all incidents in writing and reporting them to your superior. If your harasser is your boss, go higher. But if there is nowhere higher to go, then leaving may be your best option and, if appropriate, contacting an attorney is a step to take before or after you leave. Document all incidents including the time, date, events, conversations and any witnesses. There is no room for sexual harassment in the workplace. Not yesterday, not today, not ever.

Stick up for yourself when dealing with jerks

Having a job does not mean that you're a doormat. Not everybody in the workplace is kind and fun. Some real jerks have jobs at unexpected places. Sometimes they are just jerks—people who respond inappropriately or rudely, especially to your face or within earshot—but sometimes their bad behavior or meanness has nothing to do with your interactions with them. Maybe their son was just diagnosed with cancer and they are angry with the world. Maybe they had to work incredibly hard for every opportunity and everything they have and are jealous because life appears to be easy for you.

Who knows why they are jerks? Just be kind, gracious and get away from them as soon as you can.

For example, if someone on your work team humiliates you by rudely complaining that you didn't do the job right and clearly don't know what you're doing, you can say, "With your help and advice, I'll overcome my newness and learn how things are done here." That's much better than shrinking into the background or running to the restroom and crying. It says, "I belong here just as you do. Give me a chance and I'll do it right or at least the way you want it."

Listen to your gut

If you feel uncomfortable about a meeting or potential job interview, listen. Harvey Weinstein in his bathrobe opening the door would be enough to make most of us flee in the other direction. Yet how many intelligent young actresses fell for his trap? Did they really believe that they were going to be "interviewed" or have a meeting in his hotel room?

Sometimes a scenario seems totally innocent but isn't. Let's say your meeting or job interview is scheduled to take place over lunch at a restaurant at a nice hotel, as your interviewer is attending a conference there. Should you be wary? Perhaps. Hotels are easy places for novice employees or applicants to be led astray in the hopes of landing a promotion or a job. If you are invited to a hotel lunch, you can always suggest a nearby restaurant that is not in the hotel. "I understand that Louie's Italian House has the best fresh pasta in town, and it's on the same block. Let's try that. I'll meet you there." And you can always directly say, "I'd prefer not to meet at the hotel." If the person in charge has a problem with that, too bad.

If you are invited to lunch or dinner related to doing business or having an interview, that can be a good thing, as eating with people helps to build a bond. If it's just the two of you and dinner is suggested, just say that you are not available but can meet for lunch or coffee, where it's easier to escape if things go wrong, and simple to stay if they are right.

Starbucks is much better for a meeting or interview than a bar. Mixing cocktails with business is not a good idea for so many reasons. If your host suggests wine or alcohol, just say no. This is work, not pleasure. You have good instincts. Now use them. You can have a glass of wine when you get home.

And what about touching? Here the rule is: Other than a handshake or elbow bump, no touching is allowed in business. When someone touches you, they may be trying to create a connection, but in today's world, touching is not okay. Getting and keeping a job has nothing to do with touching in any way. If you happen to receive a stray touch, it's best to respond quickly. "Please, I don't like to be touched." That's it. No need to apologize.

Ask yourself...if you are made to feel uncomfortable as part of the interview process, is this a place you want to work?

Steer clear of potentially problematic situations

A favorite newspaper masthead of mine says: "If you don't want it printed, don't let it happen!" When you avoid all appearances of impropriety, you offer the gossips nothing to discuss. It's important to think through what you may be getting into before you get into it.

For example, you have choices about where you go and with whom you go there. Do you really want to view your co-worker's addition to his art collection or are you better off saying, "Please show me a photo." You understand. Make the smart choices every time.

Beware the workplace romance

It's great to develop friendships at work and some may lead to relationships, but be careful. Often, when employees begin to develop a relationship and one is fired, the other leaves, too, so employers generally do not want employees to be romantically connected. Some workplaces have policies that openly discourage romance in the workplace. If your romantic partner is at a higher level than you, they may keep their job while you are asked to leave. Employers differ widely in these matters, so before falling deeply in love with a work associate, check the employee handbook.

Before you connect romantically with the people where you work, you should also ask yourself if you really want romance interfering with your job and your potential there. A good question is: If I met this person outside of work, introduced at a party or by a friend, would I be interested? Thinking things through from this point of view may help you unravel some complicated issues.

Keep things to yourself

While you may love having friends, remember that the less you share with them about your work and workplace the smarter you are. When Mary Ackermann Gaer gained her real estate license, she quickly realized that some of her best friends were now her competitors. "I don't want to reveal anything that would affect my clients or my business," she says. Your ability to keep your work and workplace confidential is a golden asset.

Avoid spending too much time in the wrong place

You may make a wrong choice or take a job you really don't want because you simply need a job. You'll survive, but your life may not be as fun or exciting, and you'll lose time and energy you can't get back. Imagine that instead of working in oceanography, your dream, you apply your background in science to work as a lab clinician for a medical practice. The people you'll meet will most likely revolve around your work world, which is now the medical world, not the ocean world. They will become your close friends.

You'll go to their parties and their weddings. You may know them for life and may even marry one and stay where you are for a lifetime. And while that's fine, it's not the world you planned on. It's not a world of people who love the ocean and its dolphins and whales and moods. It's not people who love getting wet and traveling in boats to faraway places. It's a world of people who work in labs on research or in the medical world. So, your life will change.

As the Rolling Stones say, "You can't always get what you want, but sometimes you get what you need." It may be important for you to take a job in order to pay the bills, but just remember to keep your eye on what you want and don't give up. Opportunity is out there for the seekers, so remain a seeker.

Chapter 11
Work and Live a Smart Lifestyle

Keep your eye on your vision for yourself and your life.
Remain flexible enough to roll with changes in your work and your
world.

Recognize that you are much more than your resume

Life is a mix of mind, body and spirit. When you engage yourself daily in all three, you become a powerful being.

Remaining in touch with your physical being and your presence on the larger planet will help you maintain perspective that the world is far larger than just you. Taking daily walks is an excellent way to accomplish this. Walk longer each day and keep track of how long you've walked, how far you've gone and how you feel. If you have a smartphone, it contains a program and tracking device to make this simple by recording your progress by day, week, month and year. Keeping track of results makes the difference. Give it a try.

Learning to meditate will help you de-stress and focus, as will yoga. It's important to unwind your mind. Who knows, you may get hooked for life! Online or at the local sports club or gym, you will find a variety of other programs to strengthen and bring peace to your body and your mind. Tae Kwon Do, Judo, Jujitsu, Qigong are mind and body integrated practices offered in most communities.

Staying fit is a signal to your employer that you are taking care of yourself. That translates into taking care of your work and focusing on your performance. The flip side is the question in your employer's mind: "If my employee doesn't take care of themself, how will they take care of my business?"

In just thirty seconds at the beginning of any job interview or important appointment, it's your challenge to fold all of the pieces of you into one person who is self-confident enough to be interesting to your interviewer and fully present to be interested in them. When you are at ease in your mind and body, you can do this.

Pursue your interests and try new things

You won't need to set your passions aside because you are working. Quite the contrary...now is the time to pursue them more than ever! Set aside specific time to do so. You may wish to add your personal special activities to your calendar to be sure that, instead of just going home tired at the end of the day, you remember in advance that it's game night at your friend's house. You can use evenings, weekends and vacations to learn and experiment.

Perhaps your dream is to paint and take your vacations in Laguna Beach during the Plein Aire festival, or you're a technology enthusiast and finally have the vacation time and money to travel to Comdex in Las Vegas. Perhaps you've always wanted to work for the local food bank on Thanksgiving or go to Guatemala for a week as a homebuilding volunteer to feel what it's like to work on a team that helps a community.

Maybe you'd like to get behind the counter in your friend's spice shop for a weekend to experience retail and gain insight into whether owning your own shop would be right for you. If you ski or want to learn, could you join a weekend ski club? Do you love to cook? Sign up for a local cooking class or use your cooking skills to host casual dinner parties with your friends. Go for a hike on a local nature trail. Take an online course on "watercolor for beginners." Plant a garden. Join a weekend bicycling club. It's a huge world full of fun, and fun is what you need in order to stay refreshed and work even better.

The physically stronger and healthier you get, the mentally stronger and tougher you will be.

Look forward

In skiing, standup paddle boarding and many other sports, the secret is to look where you are going, not down at your feet. When you watch equestrian show jumping, you see that riders are looking ahead, moving their momentum forward with the horse. Work and success in life are like participating in sports. Keep your eye on the prize and you'll keep moving toward it.

Mary Ackermann Gaer believes in writing down her goals because, "When you see them in writing, they will happen." For the same reason she also suggests keeping an image board of things you like. When you visualize things, you move toward them.

When it comes to work, millions of details can keep you awake at night if they are all that you see. If, however, you can see your goal and your progress, the details become items to check off of your list.

Be of good spirit

Let this thought, "be of good spirit," guide you throughout the day and you will never have a bad day.

Why be of good spirit? Because people love people who smile. With a great smile you can go anywhere. Just look in the mirror, smile at yourself and see what happens. Your eyes sparkle. Your posture and attitude change.

Practice important phone calls while looking in the mirror. Better yet, make them while looking in the mirror and smiling when you're on the call. The smile comes through in your voice. You'll get the appointment for the important meeting or the seat at the table that you covet. Good things happen when you smile. You are the right person in the right place at the right time.

Save today for your freedom tomorrow

Now that you're working, it's time to start saving. The golden rule is to save 10% of each paycheck and no less. This is 10% of the "gross amount" before taxes and other things are subtracted. At your job and through most banks and credit unions, you can arrange for your paychecks to be automatically deposited into your checking account, with a specified amount going into your savings account. When you never see that money, it's much easier to avoid spending it.

If your firm offers profit sharing or 401(k) plans, learn all about them and take advantage of any for which you are eligible. They are another ticket to more money in your savings account!

I'm not a financial advisor, but I've observed that life is best when you live without debt and can enjoy and experience the things you want.

Once you have money you can do things your way. You can say no to things you don't want to do and yes to things you do.

Be ready to go to any type of event at the drop of a hat

"Buy an outfit for every type of occasion so that you have it ready," Colby Fisher Dailey advises. "This allows you to go anywhere at any moment."

Once you are started on a career, you may get the opportunity to travel. As that happens, be ready for anything. Here are a few tips to help you be ready to go on a minute's notice:

- **Always have some clean clothes** and stay ahead of laundry and cleaning.
- **Start a system of spares** to save you from emergency runs to the store. Have a backup for everything. Two toothpastes, for example, so that once you open one, you buy another spare.
- **Keep a fully packed "go" kit** with toiletries, makeup and prescription drugs. The day you return home, replenish all of the supplies and place the kit back on the shelf...

no last-minute slopping to fill miniature shampoo bottles or facing the terror of having no deodorant!

- **Keep your passport current.** If you don't have a passport, get one. That very act will open new vistas in your mind.

Staying ready to go takes work at the start, but once you create a system, you are always prepared when unanticipated events sweeten your life. What you can't do is let things go. If you wait till the last minute to do your laundry, pay your rent or handle your credit card bill, then the first time you are asked to take an unexpected trip you'll wish you had put a better system in place.

Take all of your vacation and use it to travel

Roz Savage espouses travel for everyone. "You've got to get away from the day-to-day," she says. "Travel allows more room for serendipity, chance conversations, a freshness of new ideas and experiences. If you're on the same train with the same people every day, there's no room for freshness. So many people don't try things."

If you can't afford to take a big trip to somewhere far, far away, plan a shorter trip to somewhere closer to home. But do find a way to travel.

Using travel to ease into a total change of career from management consultant to ocean rower, Roz quit her job and traveled for 3-1/2 months around Peru. "I couldn't have done the ocean rowing without my travel experience," she explained. Travel took her from a fixed mindset to a growth mindset. "Once I knew I had the skills, I had the self-belief."

Are you in the trap of believing that you are essential and that if you take a vacation, the world at your place of work will fall apart? Don't be. Ever. It's your time to renew and refresh!

Travel light

On my first business trip with a group, I was the person that needed to go to baggage to await my luggage when everyone else had their bag in hand, glaring at me because they had to wait instead of jumping into a taxi.

I quickly learned how to pack a week's worth of business, semi-formal wear and sometimes cowboy boots in a carry-on bag. Here is my formula for what goes into that bag:

- 1 suit jacket
- 1 matching or dark skirt
- 1 or 2 pairs of dark pants
- 3 tops, including a crisp white shirt
- 2 scarves
- 2 sets of shoes
- 1 pair of jeans, shorts or leggings
- 1 swimsuit
- Underwear for several days
- 1 ready-to-go bag of toiletries, makeup and personal items

I wear my coat and/or heavy or bulky items on the plane.

For a formal or evening look, I include a satiny eggshell-colored blouse that sets off my suit jacket, and a simple necklace and earrings. Unless it's a very special event, I leave the expensive jewelry behind and wear good-looking costume jewelry instead. No one knows.

Travel light and emerge from the plane like Kendall Jenner in shades, wrapped in an amazing coat or a shawl accented by a fabulous scarf that was in your handbag. It's easy.

Be cautious when you travel

It's your trip and you want some say or control over when you arrive and where you stay, especially if you are traveling alone. Once, in an attempt to save money, a well-meaning but inexperienced assistant booked me in the wrong part of Chicago. I had not told her directly, "I'd like to stay within three blocks of the convention center and would like to approve the hotel before you book it." Fortunately, I was with another employee and we traveled in a wolfpack of two, but I learned to be specific after that.

I also recommend that you arrive during daylight hours. It's good to know where you are. If you want to get some fresh air you can always ask the front desk or hotel concierge where it is safe to walk or run. If they warn against, listen, and use the hotel gym instead.

Lock and chain the door whenever you are in your room. Don't let anyone in. If someone says they're from the hotel staff, ask for ID and call the front desk. Use your head. Look around you. Watch for people who don't belong. Don't bring strangers back to your hotel no matter how nice they may seem. I'm not paranoid, but if I've seen something or someone I don't like, I'll ask Security to escort me to or from my room.

Be smart about social events and alcohol

Drinking like the gals in "Bridesmaids" is really not the best idea. You can like them, but don't be like them. And be careful about posting party photos on social media, too. Your prospective employers are bound to find them.

The antithesis of the gals in Bridesmaids was a lady named Diana, Princess of Wales, also known as Her Royal Highness and the mother of Princes William and Harry. Always cheeky and very well dressed, Diana had her own way of handling the toasts that came with the tiara. I've read that at events, she'd ask for her wine glass to be discreetly filled with water so that she could toast all night long. No one knew the difference between her water and the white wine.

Just remember at work events and social occasions that there is more wine on the planet and you can always have a glass at home, far away from the ability to say or do the wrong thing. It works.

Stay ahead of everyday things

Here are some simple tips for ensuring that everyday things don't derail you...

- **If you have a car, keep at least a half tank of gas in it at all times** so that when you are asked to run a quick errand, you actually can. Try filling up every Saturday. It works.

- **Always show up looking great** even if you went to a big concert 90 miles away the night before. The day you don't do this, you'll end up someplace wishing you looked a lot better.
- **Wear or bring a great jacket** or keep a scarf in your bag so that you can dress up an outfit in a flash.
- **Carry a backup charger for your cell phone** and make sure it's always full charged.
- **Schedule your next hair appointment** on the way out the door from this one. That way you will always look your best.
- **Get a full-length mirror** so that you can see how you look from head to toe in every outfit.
- **Take great care of yourself** in body, mind and spirit. Every day!

Chapter 12
Know When to Move On

*In every job, including your starter job, spend enough time to learn,
gain experience and network, and then be sure to evaluate
before you go.*

Exercise your sense of adventure

You're young. You are going to do what you want. You'll get a good job with good mentors to learn important things, but you don't need to stay forever. Satisfy the piece of you that is you, and you can live with yourself for the rest of your life.

I am hoping that you are not burdened with student debt or expensive mortgages or confining relationships and that if you are, you can at least lift the flap of the tent that confines you to see what's outside. And then go there for a while.

You may be young with possibilities in front of you that won't last. After two years of experience, you may be ready to test your own waters to see where to put in your boat and find where it floats. Remember, it's your life and your career. It's okay to question and to explore. Life is to be experienced!

Be careful about making long-term commitments before you really know who you are as an adult and what you want for yourself and your career. Your flexibility is your lifeline.

Trust yourself when you believe it's time to move on

You'll know. You'll just know. I recently received a request for a letter of recommendation from an excellent employee at the arts organization I ran. She's smart and talented at running special events. Under her guidance, the events have grown and so has the income they produce. Likely, if she wanted to stay for the next ten years, she'd have her job or perhaps a better one as a company executive.

Yet she's ready to leave. It's not a salary issue, as she's very well paid. It's not a boss issue, as she runs her department and reports only to the top. It's a personal issue: It's time for her to grow. She's ready to learn new things and explore new environments, and I applaud her.

Likewise, after eight years of growing as business manager of a large design firm, it was hard for Tiana Webb Evans to leave. She knew that if she stayed, she'd stay forever, and she'd already reached the highest point. "There was no one from me to learn from," she relates, "and I knew that at 30, I was clear there was so much more to learn and many more adventures to be had."

You know it's time to go when you are no longer excited to go to work for several weeks in a row. Work is up and down. Everyone experiences that. However, if you are starting to become bored, depressed or just miserable, it's time for self-evaluation. You're not fooling anyone. Co-workers pick up on your vibe and bosses do, too.

You must ask, it is me or is it the situation? If it's me, what can I do? Bring more excitement into my life? See a therapist? Start to exercise? Spend more time with friends? But if it's genuinely your work that's bringing you down, then it may be time for a change. Can you talk with your boss and ask for an assignment in an area where you are more challenged? Or fix whatever is bothering you? That's worth exploring before leaving. However, there is no need to suffer silently in a job. Most things can be fixed. But not all.

"It all adds up in the end," says Jennifer Slaughter. "No piece in a career is insignificant. If something doesn't work out, you know it and move on."

That said, an emotional event is rarely the right reason to move on.

Sometimes you'll want to go because something happens at work that seems unbearable or embarrassing or humiliating. It's tough, but that's the nature of working with other people. Things happen. You make mistakes. Someone calls you out on something and you just want to die and run home and pull the covers over your head and never get up again much less get up the next morning and go back to work. But you get over it. If you're tough, and you really must be to work in today's world, then you'll be okay. Maybe you'll be sheepish the next morning but soon you will be back in the groove. And then the "incident," whatever it was, will eventually fade into the background and be forgotten.

For a few brief minutes, though, you felt like quitting. Congratulations for not doing so, as you are not a quitter and you want control over how you leave. You would like the time and opportunity to plan your exit, not just react to a situation at work. How you leave matters. Relationships matter. And it's hugely important to keep relationships intact because the people you work for and with can be the references or networkers you will need when applying for your next job. Down the road, when you are applying for Job #3, your old boss and your co-workers may prove to be invaluable!

Aim to stay for at least two years

Your first job is most likely going to be a "starter job." If possible, you should stay for at least two years. Here's why:

- **It takes one year to learn a job,** to go through all of the phases of the work and become experienced and competent (see "the Hell Curve" in Chapter 7). Your employer has invested in teaching and training you and you have value to them and the company. Plus, it's likely that after you know a job, you'll have more fun. While you're always learning, in your second year you'll do a lot more doing and growing. Likely you'll have more responsibilities and challenges.
- **You don't want to be seen as a job-hopper.** Prospective employers reviewing your resume will notice how frequently you change jobs. They may be more motivated to invest in you when you have spent at least two years at your prior position. Job-hoppers are usually poor

investments. They drain the energy out of a business. To most employers, employee turnover represents money out the door.

If you're in a good job and things are going well, think carefully about leaving. I've heard from many former employees that they were in too big a rush and didn't realize how good they had it, especially at their first jobs.

If you believe you can go back after you leave, you're fooling yourself no matter what your employer has said to you. You can rarely go back. Most employers don't rehire an employee who has resigned from a good job because they are likely to resign all over again. So, in most scenarios, you won't be rehired unless to take a very different job.

Take action if you have a toxic boss

If you have a toxic boss, that's a tough one. Work as long as you can. Watch what's going on around you to determine if the issue is between the two of you or broader than that. If it's between the two of you, schedule a meeting in a very neutral place to talk. If that won't work, then just meet. Don't let things build up. Be well prepared to discuss your observations about what's going on, put it on the table and listen. Take time later to think about the conversation before you act.

If your boss won't meet or you believe that you are not being treated fairly in seeking their time and receiving a response, you may have to go up a level to get help and clarity. It's possible that your boss' superior will bring the two of you together in a meeting of the three of you to talk things out and create a path to get back on track. Good bosses listen to both sides in a dispute and help the parties come to resolution.

Be yourself

You have hopes and aspirations and you are the only person on the planet who knows if your chimes are ringing because you're thrilled every day with your role at work and your career. It's imperative that you listen to your inner self and sense of values. You be you.

Here are some things to think about:

- **Are you valued at work?** It's also important that you receive positive feedback for jobs well done, and that your compensation reflects your value.
- **Can you grow in your job?** If you ask for more challenges, will you get them?
- **Do you like and enjoy your team environment?** Do you work in a universe of professionalism, respect and encouragement?
- **Do you have the amount of adventure and excitement that you desire?** If life is a drudge, you may be ready for a big change.

You have a spark. You have dreams. If you are not feeling confident, happy and inspired for an extended period of time, take a long weekend dedicated exclusively to YOU and spend quiet time thinking about who you can be and what steps you will take to get there. Leave the friends, family members and partners behind so that you can take walks, savor a cup of coffee or tea and think.

Write down your goals and dreams. When you write, you are making a commitment. Then make the plan to get from where you are to where you want to go—with your good reputation and relationships intact. Then execute your plan.

Know what you want from something before you pursue it. And know when it's time to move on.

Do you need to have the next job lined up? Might you consider graduate school if you are uncertain about your career path but clear about your areas of interest? Only you can answer these things. It is always easier to make these choices and changes when you are free of major commitments. How you leave your current job depends on your personality, your finances, your ability to roll with things and, really, what works best for you. It's important that you believe the timing is good unless you are simply asked to leave. Then you have no control, so leave quickly and leave what you can in good order.

A simple way to look at things comes from ocean rower Roz Savage. When she was trying to decide whether to answer the call to adventure and embark on the ocean, she asked herself, "What's the best thing that can happen? What's the worst thing that can happen?" For Roz, as she was tossed from wave to wave in a storm, the answer to the latter was a bit dismal...it meant going to the bottom of the sea! Most of your choices won't have such severe consequences.

Leave professionally...always

It's simple. Write a good resignation letter, less than a page, and hand it to your boss.

In the letter, be sure to thank your boss and the company for what you have learned and the good experiences you have had. If your boss has been a good mentor, then say so. You don't need to provide details about why you are leaving or where you are going, but you can. Just end with a nice thank you.

Give two weeks' notice and no more. Two weeks' notice is "industry standard" and ample time to tie up loose ends. You owe that to an employer that's been good to you. Give no more than two weeks' notice unless you are contractually committed to do so. Don't tell your co-workers that you are giving notice. Let your boss be the first to know and the one to announce it. Then, after two weeks, be gone.

Employees "in transition" are toxic to a workplace. Co-workers don't want to pull you into meetings anymore, especially if the meetings have to do with the future. After all, you won't be there.

Your ego may try to tell you that you are so important that they'll never replace you. Of course, they won't, but it's possible that they'll have someone with different skills and a more crooked smile sitting in your cubicle within a week.

In some industries, especially financial industries and gaming, all you have to do is mention that you'll be leaving, and you'll be escorted to clean out your desk, asked for your keys and shown the door.

Once you announce that you are leaving, go gracefully. And don't return to visit until at least a year has passed. They'll move on and so will you!

Conclusion
Create the Life You Want

Be all of who you are and can be. Create a beautiful life for yourself.

Catch the good waves

My husband Larry is a surfer. For my 45th birthday he taught me how to surf. If you haven't tried, I highly recommend it.

There is something philosophically satisfying about surfing. First, it's the idea of waiting for waves. Surfing requires sitting on a board in the ocean waiting for waves. Some days, they come and come and come. Some days, they are few and far between. But in between the waves, you're out there on a board feeling the water under you as it licks your legs and you are afloat in nature, feeling atop the world. You hear the water and the wind. You see the land from your perch on your board. And you are in touch with yourself because you'd be foolish not to be in the now when you have an opportunity like this.

There's a lot to this issue of waiting for waves. You wait for the good ones because if you don't, you'll be wasting your energy on small, unworthy ones. It takes a lot of strength to paddle out from shore to where the big waves are, and it's not to be wasted on dinky ones. You only take the "cruisers," the waves large enough to catch, because otherwise you'll end up in the surf near shore exhausted but needing to paddle out once more. So, you only spend energy on the good ones. And that means waiting. And discretion. Because waves come in "sets," usually sets of three. The first wave of the set is smaller than the following two. And you have to catch the wave you choose with momentum. You frantically paddle as the wave is coming, not as it arrives, so as to be ahead of it in order to catch it.

And once you do catch that big wave, you're in for the thrill of a lifetime as you stand on your board and the surf churls under your feet and carries you like a goddess to shore. Nothing in the world compares.

Lifetime opportunities come in sets, too. Sometimes one appears on the horizon as a job that looks good and requires your momentum to catch it, only to have it fizzle out beneath you. But the good ones are worth waiting for and catching as they come through.

Catching the small, inadequate waves is exhausting, as is working in the wrong jobs or just having a job to have a job. If you can wait to catch the right waves, and I know that often you cannot, the payoff can be huge.

When you reach the point in your career when you can wait for the big waves, you've made it!

Enjoy a rich and fulfilling life...you can do it!

When you start your career you are learning the tools and techniques required to propel you further to take you where you want to go. You may have no idea of where you are headed but it sorts itself out if you remain true to yourself. Without even knowing, if you are persistent at putting one foot ahead of the other and not being discouraged or deterred or settling for things you don't want, you will find out.

To those who shared their knowledge with me, I am forever grateful. My life is rich with ideas, people, travel and opportunities as a result.

Yours can be, too. Start in the right place, with intention. Follow that up with persistence, not being knocked down regardless of circumstances or failures. Trust your intuition. And save as you go so that when opportunities present themselves, you can take them!

Start charting your path now

Let's do that exercise of Roz Savage's—writing your obituary. In fact, let's start two of them right now.

The first obituary will describe the woman you will be if you stay on a path that is comfortable but not right for you... perhaps what your parents and others want you to do. "Emiko worked at the hospital for X years, married her high school sweetheart, James, and had three children. Her children are grown and live in the same town. She was active in the book club at the women's league." You understand where I am going here. What does your obituary look like if you do the "right" things for others but the wrong things for you, putting your real feelings in a box and proceeding on the path that others have chosen for you?

The other obituary is of you on fire. It imagines that you launched your own rocket and did the things of your dreams. "Emiko became a Naval aviator and professional photographer. Her aerial photos are published in a best-selling coffee table book. She was married to the Arctic adventurer Tim Asakura. Their three children are grown and pursuing adventures of their own." And more.

You'll like the second obituary. Write it now and keep it. And get going.

Your first jobs are your first steps to open the door to a whole new world where you create the life of your dreams. It's up to you to make it happen...and Yes! You can do it!

Appendix 1: Personal Inventory

Gain clarity about how much you bring to an employer.

What do I know how to do?	What skills does this require?	What skills or attributes does this show that will benefit my employer?
Mow the lawn, plant a garden	Applying physical coordination and strength Troubleshooting a lawnmower engine Planting the flowers	Mowing – I have patience and persistence Engine – I know how to make things work Gardening – I like to design how things look
Babysit	Patience Kindness Attention Problem-solving Flexibility Sense of humor	I love kids and people I can roll with situations as they arise I am highly responsible, reliable and trustworthy I have fun
Design websites	Knowledge of technology Working with others to get their ideas Attention to detail Creativity	I understand technology I am a good listener and communicator I see things through I bring my creative self to tackling projects

Wait tables	Teamwork with the chefs and crew Ability to work with the public Working with money Customer service Positive attitude	I am a team player I work well with customers I can handle financial transactions I am a positive person
Now it's your turn...		

Appendix 2: Personal Career Map

Use this simple tracking tool.

The Personal Career Map is designed to help you evaluate your skills and likelihood of getting specific careers based upon where you are right now. It will help you form a realistic picture of what you may need to do to get started in a new career area.

Here's how it works...

Make a list of all of the possible careers or jobs you are considering, as well as those that you dream of. Remember, this is a tool to see where you can go and what it will take to get there.

Now assign each career choice a letter—A, B, C and so on. You'll use the letter to locate the career on the Career Map.

Gabriella's Personal Career Map

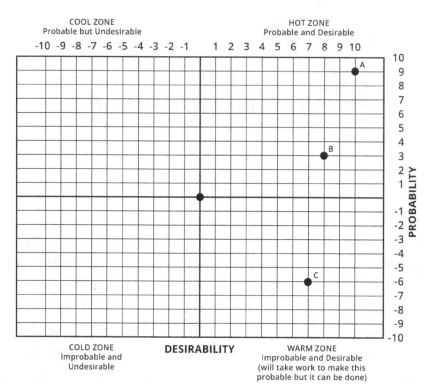

Gabriella's Career Choices:

A. Advertising Executive

B. Publicist for NY Fashion House

C. Horse Trainer

D. _____

E. _____

F. _____

G. _____

H. _____

I. _____

J. _____

For example, let's look at Gabriela's map and chart her top choices. Choice A for Gabriela is Advertising Executive. Gabriela has some good entry-level qualifications in her background. She:
- Worked as an intern at an ad agency
- Has a reference letter from the president of that firm
- Was a journalism major in college, with a minor in advertising
- Was a reporter on the campus newspaper in college
- Was vice-president of the college marketing club

Based on this experience it makes sense for Gabriela to believe that it is probable she will get job interviews from ad agencies. She would therefore rank this job 10 for desirability and a 9 for probability and would situate the letter A in the upper right-hand corner of the chart at the intersection where the 10 and 9 meet, in the hot zone. Gabriela would be almost sure of a job in her field: She has maximum desire and outstanding qualifications.

What can boost the probability of Gabriela's ending up as an advertising executive? Likely some or all of these things:
- Landing an entry-level job at an ad agency where she can work her way up
- Getting an informational interview with an ad executive to find out more about the industry and what skills are currently needed in the industry
- Joining the local ad club where ad professionals meet
- Going to an online university or night school to acquire additional skills needed in the industry and getting back in touch with the ad executive to tell them what she is doing

All of these will boost Gabriela's career goal choice. They take work but can bring a big payoff.

Let's look at another of Gabriela's career interests. Gabriela's Choice B is a job as publicist for a New York fashion house. Her entry-level qualifications for this job include:

- A personal interest in fashion combined with her good sense of style
- Her journalism and college newspaper experience

At this time Gabriela lives in Cleveland and has no experience in the world of fashion. For her to work in New York she would need to move at least initially to gain immersive experience in the fashion world.

When Gabriela entered this career choice, she gave it an 8 for desirability and a 3 for probability. It therefore falls in the hot but not hottest part of the Career Map. Why? Because although Gabriela may believe that this is a glamorous job, she has little real experience or professional knowledge in the world of fashion publicity and no contacts in place to help her. The probability of her landing this type of job in New York is slim without considerable work on her part. It is unlikely that a company will pay for Gabriela to interview or relocate to New York when lots of qualified candidates can be found nearby.

In order for Gabriela to move this career choice into a hot zone, she can:

- Take courses on business and fashion marketing online or at a community college
- Move to New York and start networking
- Take a job in fashion in Cleveland to gather skills and experience
- Or do something similar or more radical. And if this is her dream, why not?

Gabriella has fantasized throughout her life about being a horse trainer. She has:

- Ridden one week a year on family vacations
- Worked as a "hand" in cleaning and taking care of horses at her local stable
- Watched horse training programs on You Tube

When she goes to map this career choice, though it is high in desirability, it is low in probability without a lot more real-world experience to be gained on her part. Gabriella will need to:

- Become an excellent rider and teacher
- Learn much more about horses, including anatomy, behavior and medicine
- Enroll in an equine learning program, perhaps at a college or community college
- Find a good mentor who is a trainer

She'll map this career as a 7 in desirability and a -6 in probability, placing it in her warm zone as desirable but not currently probable, knowing that it will require a tremendous amount of work to achieve. If it's the career she really wants for her life, she will have a realistic view of what it may take to succeed.

Now it's your turn. You can map several careers on one chart and get a head start on your dreams. This chart is also available for download from my website, www.NancyWilhelms.com.

My Personal Career Map

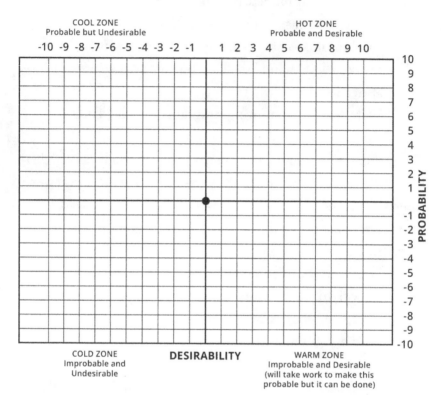

COOL ZONE
Probable but Undesirable

HOT ZONE
Probable and Desirable

-10 -9 -8 -7 -6 -5 -4 -3 -2 -1   1 2 3 4 5 6 7 8 9 10

PROBABILITY

COLD ZONE
Improbable and
Undesirable

DESIRABILITY

WARM ZONE
Improbable and Desirable
(will take work to make this
probable but it can be done)

My Career Choices:

A.

B.

C.

D.

E.

F.

G.

H.

I.

J.

Appendix 3: Examples about Me

Complete this simple chart in order to have examples
for easy reference.

I knew I had courage when

_____

_____

I was being authentic and true to myself when

_____

_____

I exhibited flexibility when

_____

_____

I grew my self-confidence by

_____

_____

I acted with integrity when

_____

_____

I was a team player when

_____

_____

I collaborated with others to accomplish something greater than all of us when

_____

_____

I used my creatively when

_____

_____

I knew I would keep learning for a lifetime when

_____

_____

Appendix 4: Your Resume

The ticket to your exciting career.

As a recent graduate you are a junior-level candidate for jobs. Since you do not yet have much experience, keep your resume to one page.

Prospective employers will be looking at your education, internships (if applicable), experience and interests. You should:

- Place your education at the top of your resume. Include any degrees you have obtained as well as any academic honors.
- List your internships, but don't go into much detail. You will want to list only tasks that may be important in your field.
- Include your extracurricular activities, the things that tell the story of who you are, your interests and accomplishments.

Be sure that your resume is easy to read and contains lots of white space. You don't need many details, but you do need to use bullet points and action verbs to make it stand out. If you have references, just say, "References available on request."

For more information about resumes, also see Chapter 3.

Sample Resume

Issa James
1097 Webster Circle
Milwaukee, WI 53211
Cell: (414) 782-9334
issajoyjames@gmail.com
www.issajoyjames.com

EDUCATION
University of Wisconsin–Madison
B.A. in Political Science, minor in Family Studies (GPA 3.8), 2019
Academic Honors
Dean's List

WORK AND INTERNSHIP EXPERIENCE

WSMW 91.9 FM (Madison, WI)   June 2019–present
Local student-run radio station
Community Outreach Intern
- Worked with Community Outreach Director on free family concerts and art events designed to build family participation and involvement; reached 9,500 persons.
- Served as staff team member on WSMW Turkey Trot; reached 2,500 running enthusiasts with a race, health fair and concert.

Oaks Country Club (Milwaukee)   Summers 2017, 2018
Private tennis and swim club with 500 family memberships
Waitress and Banquet Team Member
- Coordinated banquet, wedding and special event teams working with the Special Events Manager
- Worked with World Tennis Association team on the Northwestern Digits Clay Courts Tournament awards banquet and TV broadcast set-up

EXTRACURRICULAR ACTIVITIES AND INTERESTS
- President of the University American Sign Language Club
- Member, Habitat for Humanity, Campus Chapter, affordable housing team
- Volunteer Server, Madison Community Food Bank, Sunday suppers
- Interest: swimming, reading, film festivals, live music, chess

Appendix 5: Your Cover Letter

The piece that really helps you stand out to get an interview and hopefully, the job.

Again, as a recent graduate, you won't have too much to say. The goal of the cover letter is to let the recruiter or interviewer know that you have done your homework and are genuinely interested in this position. Most importantly, they are looking to see that you will be a good fit for them and that you will bring the very best of yourself to this opportunity.

You will need to write a separate cover letter every time you send a resume. A resume submitted without a cover letter looks like you're "shot gunning" and will go straight to the bottom of the pile. Always submit a cover letter with your resume.

Prospective employers are looking for what YOU can do for THEM. So, this is not an "I this" and "I that" letter. It's a "you" letter. In fact, a good rule of thumb here and forever in your correspondence is: don't start a paragraph with the word "I."

Make it easy to read and let it breathe with white space. Let it be one page at most.

If you have done your homework on the company and the job, researching far beyond the simple job description, this will flow naturally. Your goal is to match what you offer with what they need.

Writing a good cover letter takes time. Expect to spend at least 1-2 hours and perhaps more to get it right. If you are willing to put your time into doing this right, your future employer is likely to believe that you will be willing to put your time into quality and excellence at work. So enjoy the process and give it your all!

Remember...Every cover letter is different. The one that follows is merely a sample. Yours will be personalized to reflect who you are and your excitement about the job, as well as what you will bring to it.

Sample Cover Letter

Issa James
1097 Webster Circle
Milwaukee, WI 53211
issajoyjames@gmail.com • www.issajoyjames.com

January 5, 2021
Ms. Amy Nelson Schmitz
Vice President of Marketing
Nimble Corporation
123 Woods Road
Milwaukee, WI 53201

Dear Ms. Schmitz:

In response to your ad for Special Events Assistant, I am pleased to submit my resume and qualifications. From your ad and the information I have found on your company, I understand that Nimble Corporation stages large events for the community as well as private events for its clients and shareholders. I believe that my experience in events, outreach and client services will be valuable to Nimble Corporation as a Special Events Assistant on its team.

As detailed in the attached resume, I most recently worked as an intern for public radio station WSMW in Madison, WI to engage community members in upbeat fun, family and cultural events in which over 12,000 people participated. We built a name for the station by delivering more than news and music. During college summers, I returned to Milwaukee to work at a private club where I participated in staging an international awards banquet and television broadcast for the Northwestern Digits Clay Courts Tournament. In both capacities, I enjoyed the challenges to be creative and to problem-solve.

My responsibilities have included events planning and implementation and managing and supervising the work of others. I understand how to create timetables and budgets in order to achieve desired results. I am self-motivated and goal-oriented and love to be part of a team dedicated to excellence and success. I will bring these qualities to my work with Nimble. This would be an outstanding opportunity for me to start my career with Nimble, a highly respected company, in work that I enjoy and a community that I love.

It would be a pleasure to talk further with you about this position. May I hear from you soon?

Thank you.
Sincerely,
Issa James

Appendix 6: Job Interview Worksheet

*The Job Interview Worksheet is designed to prepare you
to nail your interview.*

To download this worksheet go to www.NancyWilhelms.com.

Today's date:

_____

Company name:

_____

Address where I will interview:

_____

_____

_____

Interview date:

_____

Interview time:

_____

Interviewer and his/her title:

_____

Job I am interviewing for:

_____

Job responsibilities that I know of from the job posting:

_____

_____

_____

The company makes/does:

_____

_____

_____

The company's mission statement is:

_____

_____

_____

The company is known for:

_____

_____

_____

I am interested in this job and company because:

_____

_____

_____

I believe I would be a good fit for this job/company because of these unique things about me and my background:

_____

_____

_____

I have these special skills or talents that will be important in this role:

_____

_____

_____

Here is a connection that I have to this job or company:

_____

_____

Here is what I know about my interviewer (learned from reading the company's website, doing a Google name search, and searching on LinkedIn, Facebook and Instagram):
- Went to school at:

_____

- **Has been at the company since:**

_____

- **Focuses on this in his/her work:**

_____

- **Is interesting to me because:**

_____

- Questions I have about this job are:

1. _____
2. _____
3. _____
4. _____
5. _____

What I want the interviewer to know and believe about me in three key one-sentence messages is:

Example: In my summer job as a hotel concierge assistant, every day I went out of my way for customers, and I will bring that knowledge, attitude and approach to this company for the benefit of its customers.

Example: Because I went to school in Atlanta, where this job is based, I have beneficial experience from living in the South and know how to navigate the community and build relationships there.

1. _____
2. _____
3. _____

Once you have done your homework, you will have much more insight into how to link your experience to the job, the company and the interviewer. Again, be honest and don't make anything up. For example, in researching the company and interviewer you may not find a great deal of information, but your research will be invaluable in showing during the interview that you have done your homework.

Post Interview

Points I want to include in my thank you letter (to be sent within 12 hours of the interview) are:

1. _____
2. _____
3. _____

I am sending these materials that the interviewer requested:

_____

My thank you letter went out on this date:

_____

The other follow up that I will make is:

_____

OTHER NOTES

_____

_____

_____

_____

_____

Appendix 7: Obituary Exercise

You can re-imagine your life starting now!

An obituary is a notice of a person's death, usually with a short biographical account.

This exercise is about imagining your own obituary in two different ways. After you complete this exercise, be sure to date and keep it so that you can refer back to it as you fulfill your dreams. Remember, you become what you dream, so go for it!

- **Obituary Exercise #1 – If I stay on my current path:** This represents where you are headed in your life today. Pull out a sheet of paper or go to work on your computer and write a simple obituary of yourself, assuming that you continue on your current life path without major change. Imagine that on the day after your death, this is what will be read about you and your life.
- **Obituary Exercise #2 – If I pursue my dreams:** Repeat the exercise, but this time write the obituary as if you did all of the things that you are dreaming of, even if it required you to radically alter your life.

Acknowledgements

Writing and publishing this book has meant a lot to me, and I would like to thank those who have joined me on this journey.

My interviewees have made much of this book possible. It has been a pleasure to talk and work with each of you. Many thanks to Jan Anderson, Colby Fisher Dailey, Tiana Webb Evans, Mary Ackermann Gaer, Lynda Keeler, Rosalind (Roz) Savage and Jennifer Slaughter. Colby took a special role in encouraging me to share my stories and to help others as I had with her early in her career.

Thank you to my editor, Linda Coss, whose sharp mind and good observations have helped this book grow and take final form.

I extend thanks to Joe Bunting and Sarah Gribble of The Write Practice, whose systems, persistence and constant encouragement kept me on track through the initial manuscript and second draft, and who shared with me an ongoing flurry of motivational quotes to keep me pushing through to conclusion.

To my beta readers, Lisa Parry Becker and Miriam Flores, I owe a debt of gratitude for helping me make the book as good as it can be.

My tribe of friends has been a steady source of encouragement, as have my brothers, Bill and John Fisher, and my cousin, Sally Kile.

Early in my career I was fortunate to work with Nancy Gray, a mentor who immensely influenced my life and work. When asked if she employed men at her firm, Nancy, a feminist, replied, "Yes we do. We just don't pay them as much."

I learned so much from my bosses, W. Thomas MacArthur, Richard Schulze, Herbert Pastor and Governor Robert List. They encouraged me as a young woman to keep going and learn more. Ann Korologos taught me much about the non-profit enterprise, governance and how to work with a Board. David Fuente helped me grow as an organizational leader. Photographer Walter Sheffer understood the gentle side of business and was a truly unique individual who showed me that living a warm, kind and authentic life matters. I thank all of these individuals for sharing, teaching and helping me grow.

I'd like to acknowledge the roles of sports and nature in my life, in teaching me that self-challenge results in insight, and my mom, Harriet Fisher, who would take any reason to head outdoors, whether it was tennis, cross-country skiing, flying a kite or just walking.

Lastly, I would like to thank my husband for his constant support through two countries and countless kitchen tables as I wrote this book. His belief in me and this book has been invaluable.

To finish, I salute all of the young adults whose optimism brightens their eyes as they enter the work force with hopes, dreams and insights to make the world a better place for us all.

Yes! You can do it!

About the Author

Nancy Wilhelms is an author, entrepreneur, speaker and coach. Throughout her career she has mentored countless young women, helping them join the workforce and grow into leadership roles with rewarding careers. She is the founder of an award-winning global marketing communications firm and has enjoyed a fulfilling career with roles in private industry, government and non-profit organizations. Nancy believes in working hard and finding joy in all she does. She spends her time in Basalt, Colorado and Palm Springs, California and enjoys Baja Mexico.

Nancy publishes articles frequently. These are available at www.NancyWilhelms.com.